Collins need to know

Card ♥ games

All the rules and tips you need to
start playing over 60 card games

The Diagram Group

contents

Introduction

Collins need to know? Card games is a clear and
comprehensive guide to the world's most popular card
games. Inside you will find step-by-step instructions on
how to play each game, backed up with lots of colour
illustrations. There are examples of play, strategy tips and
rules for the most popular variants of each game. There
are patience (solitaire) games, games for two, three or
four players and games that can be played by four or more.

History of card games
The origins of card games are unclear. The very first purpose-made
playing cards were probably invented in China or India and were known in
Southern Europe by the end of the thirteenth century. Some scholars
believe that cards were introduced to Egypt in the eleventh or twelfth
centuries and quickly spread throughout the Islamic world, which then
included most of Spain. The concept was passed to Italy, along with many
other new ideas such as astronomy and algebra, during and after the
period of the Crusades. From Italy and Spain, playing cards quickly spread
to the rest of Europe. The four suits that are best known today – hearts,
spades, clubs and diamonds – originated in France in the sixteenth
century. In Italy, Spain and Germany playing cards with different suits are
still common. Italian and Spanish cards are marked with clubs, swords,
cups and coins, while German cards include acorns and bells alongside
the more familiar hearts and spades.

It is safe to assume that the invention of card games must have
predated the invention of playing cards, perhaps by many centuries. Some
scholars maintain that banknotes were originally used, others that small
tablets similar to dominoes were the original playing cards. Card games fall
into two broad categories: games of chance and games that require skill.
Many solitaire games and gambling games, such as Blackjack, are games
of almost pure chance. A player wins or loses depending on how well he is
able to predict the random sequence of cards produced by shuffling. Most
other games require a player to plan a strategy and to outwit his
opponents. Pure chance games are thought to be the oldest games of all
and probably developed from ancient methods of fortune-telling in which
sticks or rocks were tossed onto the ground and the patterns they formed
interpreted as favourable or unfavourable omens.

General rules and conventions

Certain aspects of card games, such as shuffling the deck or choosing a dealer, are almost universal. This section sets out rules for these basic card-playing elements that should be taken to apply to all the games in this book.

Card decks

All of the games in this book are played with the standard deck of cards used in the English-speaking world. The deck consists of 52 cards divided into four suits of thirteen cards each. The suits are spades (♠), clubs (♣), hearts (♥) and diamonds (♦) and each suit contains a King, a Queen, a Jack (or Knave), a ten, a nine, an eight, a seven, a six, a five, a four, a three, a two (or Deuce) and an Ace. Most decks also include one or two Jokers.

Some games use a smaller deck of cards, known as a 'stripped' or 'Piquet' deck, which is formed by removing all the cards below the seven (except for the Ace). Others are played with two or more full decks shuffled together and still others with two or more stripped decks shuffled together. There is an illustration in the margin on the first page of each game that tells you how many decks of cards you will need to play that game. The illustration below tells you how the cards are ranked in their suits, or refers you to the text if the ranking is complex.

These images show you how many cards you need to play a game

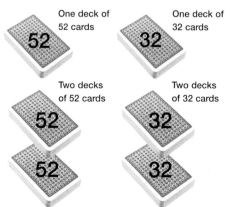

One deck of 52 cards

One deck of 32 cards

Two decks of 52 cards

Two decks of 32 cards

These images show you the standard ranking of cards in their suits

Kings high

Aces low

This information is repeated in the text

Shuffling and cutting

Before any card game, the cards should be shuffled. Cards are also usually shuffled before each deal. Convention dictates that any player involved in a game may shuffle the cards before they are given to the designated dealer. The dealer always has the right to shuffle the cards last. When shuffling cards it is important to ensure that neither you nor any other player sees the faces of any of the cards. Many people shuffle cards in such a way that they or their opponents see the bottom card of the deck as they are tidying the cards into a neat pile. It's almost impossible to 'forget' that you have seen the position of a card in the deck and it is knowledge that cannot help but affect the way you play the game. For maximum fairness and enjoyment this common mistake should be avoided.

John Scarne, the renowned card game expert who produced a guide for American GIs on how to avoid card sharps, recommended the following method of shuffling. Place the deck face-down. Lift about half the cards from the top of the deck and place them face-down next to the other half. Use your thumbs to riffle the corners of the two halves together, leaving them face-down on the table, then push the two meshed halves together. Do not take the deck off the table either when riffling or squaring off the deck; that way nobody can catch a glimpse of the bottom card.

Cutting the cards is often neglected in 'friendly' games, but it should really be done as part of the shuffling process to ensure a truly random deal. To cut a deck of cards means to divide the deck into two portions and then to transpose the position of the bottom portion with the top portion. The cards should be cut after a shuffle and the task of cutting the cards usually falls to the player on the dealer's left (assuming it is the dealer who has shuffled). This player should lift a number of cards from the top of the shuffled deck and place them face-down next to the remainder. The dealer then places the remainder on top of the removed portion to complete the cut. Care should be taken to keep the bottom card of both portions concealed at all times.

Dealing

Many games specify that cards should be dealt in 'packets'. This means that more than one card is dealt to a player before dealing to the next player. Packets are usually of two, three or four cards. For example, in a game where each player receives a total of five cards the rules may specify that they be dealt in one packet of three followed by a second packet of two. In this case, the dealer would deal three cards to the first player and then three cards to every other player before going back to the first player to deal two further cards and then another two cards to all the other players. Cards should always be dealt face-down unless the rules state otherwise.The deal usually proceeds in a clockwise direction, so that the player on the dealer's left is the first to receive cards and the dealer is the last (assuming it is a game in which the dealer receives cards). The task of dealing cards (the 'dealership') also passes in a clockwise direction, unless the rules state otherwise. In parts of the world where some of the games included in this book originate, the deal and dealership traditionally proceed in an anticlockwise direction. For the sake of simplicity these traditions have been ignored here and they make no difference to the fairness of play. No player should look at any face-down cards he has been dealt until the deal is complete.

If the dealer makes a mistake, such as dealing too many cards to one player, or allowing a card to be seen by other players, a misdeal may be declared. Any player may call for a new deal by the same dealer if he believes that a mistake has been made, but not if he has already looked at any of his face-down cards.

▼ A 19th-century Jack of clubs

Playing

Obviously each game has its own specific rules about how they should be played, but there are general points to bear in mind. Most important is the convention that players should never give away more information than is strictly necessary. This means that players should refrain from giving any indication that they have been dealt a 'good' or a 'bad' hand, or from making comments to the effect that they know which cards an opponent is looking for. This is particularly important in partnership games where players' choices are heavily influenced by considerations of which cards their partner may or may not have.

It may seem excessively strict and po-faced to insist on these restrictions, but they are important to the overall enjoyment of playing card games. The challenge of almost all card games lies in the fact that a player has limited information about the whereabouts of most of the cards in the deck. The more information a player has, the easier it is to win and there comes a point where too much information removes all the challenge from a game and renders it tedious.

games

for one

Patience or solitaire games are card games for one person. Successfully completing a patience game, especially one that relies on an element of skill, is one of the best gaming experiences.

Bisley

NUMBER
OF CARDS

52

One deck
of 52 cards

**Both Aces and Kings play the role of foundation cards in this
less than taxing solitaire that needs lots of space to lay out.**

Objective

Suits should be built in face value order onto the Aces or the Kings (the
foundation cards). Suits are built in ascending order on the Aces and in
descending order on the Kings. When the sequences meet, they are
merged together. It does not matter at which point they meet.

RANKING
ORDER

high

low

Card values

Bisley is played with a single, standard deck of 52 cards. The cards rank
in their suits with Kings highest, followed by Queens, Jacks, tens, nines,
eights, sevens, sixes, fives, fours, threes, twos and Aces (lowest).

Layout

Place the four Aces in a row face-up. The order does not matter. Deal a
further nine cards, also face-up, to the right of the four Aces to make a
row of thirteen cards. Deal out the remainder of the pack in three more
rows of thirteen cards below the first row.

EXAMPLE OF PLAY

**Example of possible play for the layout on the
opposite page:**

1 Build 2♦ onto A♦ (foundation card). 4♠ now
   available for play.
2 Build 3♦ onto 2♦. 4♣ now available for play.
3 Pack 5♦ onto 6♦. K♥ now available for play.
4 Place K♥ above A♥. K♥ now becomes a
   foundation card.
5 Pack 5♦ and 6♦ onto 7♦. 5♣ is now
   available for play.
6 Pack 5♦, 6♦ and 7♦ onto 8♦. 5♠ is now
   available for play.
7 Pack 5♣ onto 4♣. 4♥ is now available for play.
8 Pack 5♠ onto 4♠. 10♥ is now available
   for play.

BISLEY

Playing

- Initially, only the thirteen cards in the bottom row are available for play.
- A card may be built on a foundation card (at first, only the Aces) or packed on another card in the bottom row. Packing may be done onto a card that is of the same suit and that has a face value immediately below or immediately above the card to be played.
- If a King is available for play, it is placed above the Ace of the same suit and becomes available as a foundation card.
- Once a card is moved from its position in the bottom row, the card in the row above it becomes available for play. Cards may be packed in ascending or descending order of value and this can be switched at any time by the player. Continue packing and building cards until all cards are in their suit piles, or no card can be played.

MUST KNOW

Strategy tips

- It is important to free the Kings as soon as possible. The more Kings that become foundation cards, the more build opportunities you have.
- Don't lose sight of the fact that there are two sets of foundation cards. It is easy to concentrate on one and miss opportunities in the other.

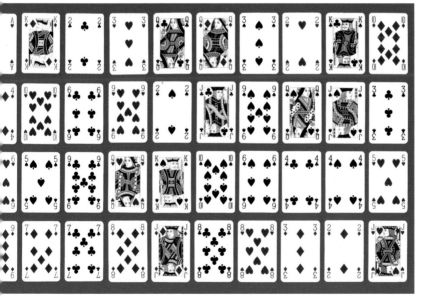

◀ Example of an initial layout

Bristol

NUMBER
OF CARDS

One deck
of 52 cards

Bristol is a patience game with a satisfying rather than taxing level of difficulty. It combines features from several other patience games.

Objective

To build sequences in ranking order on foundation Aces.

Card values

RANKING
ORDER

high

low

Bristol is played with a single, standard deck of 52 cards. The cards rank in their suits with Kings highest, followed by Queens, Jacks, tens, nines, eights, sevens, sixes, fives, fours, threes, twos and Aces (lowest).

Layout

Eight spreads of three cards each are dealt face-up. If any of those spreads contains a King, that King is placed at the bottom of that spread. Three more cards are dealt face-up below the spreads to form three reserve piles. Space is required above the spreads for a row of four Aces, which act as foundation cards when they become available. The remainder of the cards are kept face-down as the stock.

Playing

- The top card from any of the reserve piles and the exposed cards from any of the spreads are available for play.
- Aces must be played to the spaces provided for the foundation cards before sequences can be built. Once an Ace is in place, any playable card may be played to that Ace if it builds the sequence. Sequences are built on the foundation Aces irrespective of suits. For example, if the Ace of clubs has become available for play and has been placed in its position as a foundation card, any two may be played to it to build the sequence.
- Playable cards may also be built numerically upwards or downwards on any exposed card in a spread.
- When no more moves can be made with the available playable cards from the initial layout, one more card is dealt to each of the reserve piles. Any moves made available by the new cards are played and then three further cards are dealt.
- The game ends when no more moves may be made or when the four Ace-to-King sequences are complete.

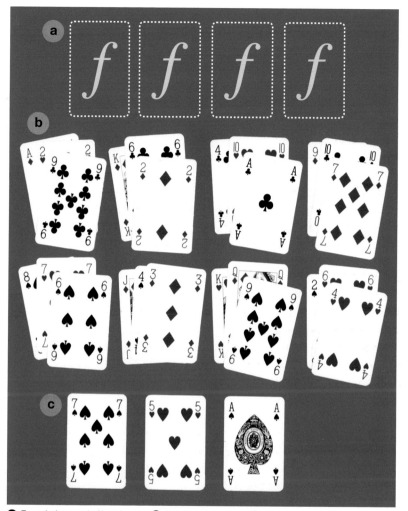

◄ Example of an initial layout

a Foundation cards (Aces) **b** Eight spreads **c** Three reserve piles

MUST KNOW

Strategy tips

• The key to completing a Bristol layout successfully is to build within the spreads in order to expose cards. Cards from the reserve piles should not generally be used to build in the spreads, except when it is necessary to expose cards buried in those piles.

• Building within the spreads also has the advantage of sorting cards into numerical sequences, which makes building on the foundation cards easier.

Clock

One deck
of 52 cards

Clock is a fast-paced and intriguing game that owes
much of its popularity to the unusual nature of its layout.
The same game is sometimes known as Sundial or
Travellers. The chances of getting all the cards out are
small, which is probably another reason why players come
back to it again and again.

Objective

RANKING
ORDER

high

low

To organise thirteen piles of cards laid out in the position of numbers on
a clock face, so that all the Aces are at the one o'clock position, all twos at
two o'clock and so on, with the Queens at the twelve o'clock position and
the Kings at the centre.

Card values

Clock is played with a single standard deck of 52 cards. The cards in their
suits rank with Kings highest, followed by Queens, Jacks, tens, nines,
eights, sevens, sixes, fives, fours, threes, twos and Aces (lowest).

Layout

The cards are dealt, one at a time and face-down, to form twelve piles
of four cards in the position of the numbers on a clock face with a
thirteenth pile in the centre of the circle. Four cards may be dealt to each
pile before moving on to the next, or each pile can be built up one card
at a time.

Playing

- The top card of the centre pile is turned over and placed next to the
appropriate pile in the circle. For example, if the first card turned over is
an eight, it is placed next to the pile in the eight o'clock position. If the first
card is a Jack, it is placed next to the pile in the eleven o'clock position.
- The top card from the pile that the last card was placed next to is
turned over and placed next to the appropriate pile in the circle. The same
thing is done with the top card of that pile and so on.
- A card may be placed next to the pile that it came from. For example,
if the top card from the pile in the eight o'clock position is turned over and
it is an eight, that card is placed next to the pile it came from and another
card from the same pile is turned over.

- Kings are placed next to the central pile and a card from that pile is turned over and placed next to the appropriate pile.
- If there are no more cards left in a pile, the card from the next pile in sequence is turned over and allocated. For example, if an eight is turned over and there are no more cards left in the pile at the eight o'clock position, a card is turned over from the pile in the nine o'clock position, or the next pile in clockwise sequence that still has cards. This will always happen when the fourth card of a particular rank is found.
- The game ends when the fourth King is turned up. If the fourth King is not the last card to be turned up, the game is lost because there is no pile next in sequence from which a card can be taken to continue the game, and no further moves may be made.

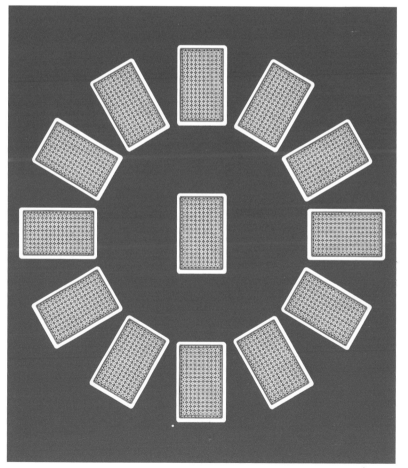

◄ Example of the initial layout

Counting

NUMBER OF CARDS

One deck
of 52 cards

RANKING ORDER

high

low

Counting, also known as Broken intervals, offers more scope for skilful play than other common patience games. A player must calculate his move at the turn of every card.

Objective

To build cards on an Ace, a two, a three and a four (the foundation cards) in ranking intervals of one, two, three and four respectively.

Card values

Counting is played with a single, standard deck of 52 cards. Cards in their suits rank with Kings highest, followed by Queens, Jacks, tens, nines, eights, sevens, sixes, fives, fours, threes, twos and Aces (lowest).

Layout

• An Ace, a two, a three and a four (from any suits) are laid out in a row on the table. These are the foundation cards. Space should be allowed above the foundation cards for four discard piles, one above each card, and space below for cards that will be built onto the layout.

• Once the initial layout has been formed, the remainder of the cards are shuffled and placed face-down on the table to form the stock.

Playing

• The topmost card of the stock is turned up and may be built onto any of the stock cards if it would contribute to one of the sequences shown in the table below:

BUILDING SEQUENCES

Foundation	Needed	Sequence
Ace	every card in rank order	A, 2, 3, 4, 5, 6, 7, 8, 9, 10, J, Q, K
two	every second card in rank order	2, 4, 6, 8, 10, Q, A, 3, 5, 7, 9, J, K
three	every third card in rank order	3, 6, 9, Q, 2, 5, 8, J, A, 4, 7, 10, K
four	every fourth card in rank order	4, 8, Q, 3, 7, J, 2, 6, 10, A, 5, 9, K

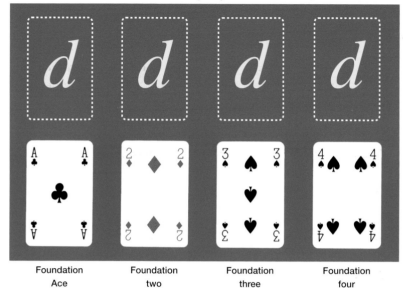

◄ Example
of an initial
layout

Foundation	Foundation	Foundation	Foundation
Ace	two	three	four

• If the first card cannot be built onto any of the foundation cards, because it does not continue one of the sequences shown in the Building sequences table on the previous page, it must be placed, face-up, on one of the four discard piles. The next card turned up from the stock is treated in the same way, and so on.

• The topmost card from any of the discard piles may be used to build any of the four sequences, but cards may not be transferred between discard piles.

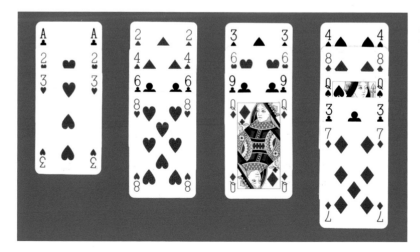

◄ Example
of sequence
building

COUNTING

19

EXAMPLE OF PLAY

Example of possible play for the layout on the previous page:

1 As the layout stands, the following cards are needed to continue building; a 4 to be built on the 3 with the Ace foundation, a 10 to be built on the 8 with the two foundation, a 2 to be built on the Queen with the three foundation, or a Jack to be built on the 7 with a four foundation. Any other card would have to be placed on one of the discard piles.

2 The next card turned up is a 4, which may immediately be built on the 3 with the Ace foundation.

3 The next card turned up is a 2, which may immediately be built on the Queen with the three foundation.

4 The next card turned up is a 5. Both the Ace-foundation sequence and the three-foundation sequence require a 5, so the player must choose one or the other (probably the Ace since it has fewer cards).

Layout after steps 2 and 3

• If a discard pile runs out of cards, a new pile may be created in its place, but there must never be more than four discard piles.

• Play continues in this manner until there are no more cards that can be played either from the discard piles or from the stock, or until a full sequence of twelve cards has been built on each foundation.

MUST KNOW

Strategy tips

• The key to successfully completing a Counting layout is to control the discard piles. This means carefully considering which discard pile you should add an unplayable card to.

• Ideally, you should place cards in the discard piles in the reverse order to the sequences. That way, you should always be able to use the top card of one of the discard piles after building with a card from the stock. If the next card needed in a sequence is buried lower down in a discard pile, it will be much more difficult to free.

• It is a good idea to place the four Kings at the bottom of one of the discard piles, since they are the four cards that will be needed to complete each of the sequences. Other sets of cards of the same rank should be scattered throughout the discard piles.

Flower garden

Flower garden is a moderately difficult patience game that gets its name from its expansive and colourful layout.

NUMBER
OF CARDS

One deck
of 52 cards

Objective

To free the four Aces and use them as foundation cards for building consecutive sequences in their suits.

Card values

Flower garden is played with a single, standard deck of 52 cards. Cards in their suits rank with Kings highest, followed by Queens, Jacks, tens, nines, eights, sevens, sixes, fives, fours, threes, twos and Aces (lowest).

RANKING
ORDER

high

low

Layout

● Six cards are dealt to six spreads which are arranged in such a way that the suit and rank of all the cards is visible and the whole of the card at the end of each spread is exposed. These six spreads are known as the 'flower beds'. Space must be left under the flower beds for four foundation cards.

● The remaining sixteen cards are arranged in another spread known as the 'bouquet'. The bouquet may be laid face-up on the table or held in the hand.

Playing

● The four Aces are removed from any of the flower beds they may have been dealt to, or from the bouquet, and placed in a row below the flower beds as foundation cards (the order does not matter).

● Any card from the bouquet or any exposed card from the ends of each of the flower beds may be built onto the foundation Ace of the same suit. The same cards may be used to build numerically upwards or downwards onto any of the exposed cards at the ends of the flower beds, regardless of suit.

● Sequences of two or more cards may also be moved from the end of one flower bed to another, as long as that other flower bed has a card that fits the sequence in the exposed position.

● When all the cards from a flower bed have been used, a single card from the bouquet, or an exposed sequence from another flower bed may be used to start a new flower bed in its place.

▶ Example of an initial layout

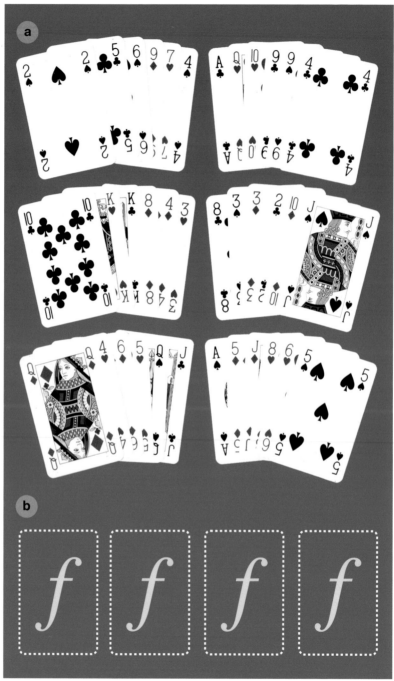

a Six flower beds (six cards each)   b Four foundation cards (Aces)

FLOWER GARDEN

22

Bouquet (sixteen cards)

EXAMPLE OF PLAY

Example of possible play for the layout on the previous page and above:

1 The A♣ and A♠ from the flower beds should immediately be placed in two of the foundation-card positions. The A♥ and A♦ should be placed in the other two positions. The bouquet now contains sixteen cards and two of the flower beds contain only five cards.

2 The 2♠ is exposed in the first flower bed and should be built on the A♠ foundation. The 5♣ is now the exposed card in that flower bed. The 2♥ and the 2♦ from the bouquet should be placed on their respective Ace foundations.

3 The 2♣ is unavailable because the 10♦ and J♠ come before it in the flower bed. To free the 2♣, the J♠ can be built on the exposed 10♣ (upward numerical build), which exposes the 10♦. The 10♦ may then be built on the exposed J♣ (downward numerical build). The 2♣ is now exposed and may be built on the A♣ foundation.

4 The twos of the relevant suits have now been built on all four foundation Aces. The 3♦ is now exposed, and building it on the 2♦ will expose the 3♠. The 3♣ is available in the bouquet, but freeing the 3♥ will require some building within the flower beds.

MUST KNOW

Strategy tips

● The key to completing a Flower garden layout successfully is to build within the flower beds in order to expose cards. Cards from the bouquet should not be used to build in the flower beds unless absolutely necessary. The more cards you can keep in the bouquet, the more cards you have free to play.

● Building within the flower beds also has the advantage of sorting cards into numerical sequences, although not within their suits, which can make building on the foundation cards easier as play continues.

Idiot's delight

NUMBER OF CARDS

One deck
of 52 cards

Idiot's delight owes its colourful name to the fact that even players with little skill have a better than fifty-fifty chance of getting all the cards out in any given deal. The same game is also known as Aces up or Firing squad.

Objective

To keep discarding cards until only the Aces are left in the layout.

Card values

RANKING ORDER

high

low

Idiot's delight is played with a single, standard deck of 52 cards. The cards rank in their suits with Aces highest, followed by Kings, Queens, Jacks, tens, nines, eights, sevens, sixes, fives, fours, threes and twos (lowest).

Layout

Four cards are dealt, face-up, in a row. As play progresses, more cards may be built up on top of these cards, but the layout does not extend across the table. The remaining 48 cards are kept as a stock. A separate discard pile is also formed.

▶ Example
of an initial
layout

IDIOT'S DELIGHT

24

Playing

● If any two of the four cards in the initial layout are from the same suit, the lowest-ranking card is removed and placed on the separate discard pile. If three or four of the cards in the initial layout are from the same suit, the two or three lowest-ranking are discarded. When a card is discarded, its place is taken by another card dealt from the stock. This process continues until all of the four visible cards are from different suits.

- When no more cards can be discarded from the initial layout, four more cards are dealt from the stock on top of the original four cards.
- The same discarding process takes place except that, when a card from the second batch of four is discarded, the card underneath it is then compared to the three remaining cards and more discards may be made. If all the cards from a pile are discarded, the space may be filled with a card taken from the top of another pile (this exposes the card underneath it for play).
- Because Aces are the highest-ranking cards, they can never be discarded. An exposed Ace can only be moved to expose the cards underneath it when a pile is exhausted and leaves a gap.
- Play continues until all the cards have been dealt. If, after the final card has been discarded, there are any cards left in the layout other than the four Aces, the game is lost.

EXAMPLE OF PLAY

Example of possible play for the layout on the previous page:

1 The 10♣, 6♦, 2♥ and 7♣ are the first cards dealt to the layout.
2 Because the 10♣ and the 7♣ are from the same suit, one of them must be discarded. The 7♣ is discarded because it is the lower-ranking card.
3 Since this is the initial deal, a new card from the stock must be added to replace the one discarded . The new card is a 7♦. There are now two diamonds in the layout so the lower-ranking, the 6♦, is discarded.
4 A new card is dealt from the stock to replace the 6♦. The new card is a 9♥. There are now two hearts in the layout so the lower-ranking, 2♥, is discarded.
5 A new card is dealt from the stock to replace the 2♥. The new card is a Q♠. Each card in the layout is now from a different suit so no more discards can be made. A second set of four cards are dealt on top of the four remaining.
6 The next four cards dealt are the J♠, 2♣, 3♦ and 6♠.

7 The 6♠ is discarded because it is a lower-ranking card than the other spade, the J♠. This exposes the 7♦ (the card beneath the 6♠ from the previous deal).

8 The 3♦ is discarded because it is outranked by the exposed 7♦. The Q♠ is exposed, which requires that the J♠ be discarded, in turn exposing the 10♣.

Layout after steps 2 to 5

Four cards of the second deal

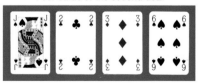

King Albert

NUMBER OF CARDS

52

One deck of 52 cards

King Albert, believed to have been named after King Albert I of Belgium, is a moderately difficult patience game that bears similarities to Klondike, except that its layout consists of face-up rather than face-down cards.

Objective

To release the Aces to act as foundation cards and then to build consecutive sequences in the same suits.

RANKING ORDER

high

low

Card values

King Albert is played with a single, standard deck of 52 cards. The cards rank in their suits with Kings highest, followed by Queens, Jacks, tens, nines, eights, sevens, sixes, fives, fours, threes, twos and Aces (lowest).

Layout

- Nine cards are dealt face-up in a row to form the basis of nine columns. A second card, also face-up, is then dealt to all the columns except the first. Each subsequent deal of seven, six, five, four, three, two and single cards is dealt to each column except for the first column dealt in the previous row.

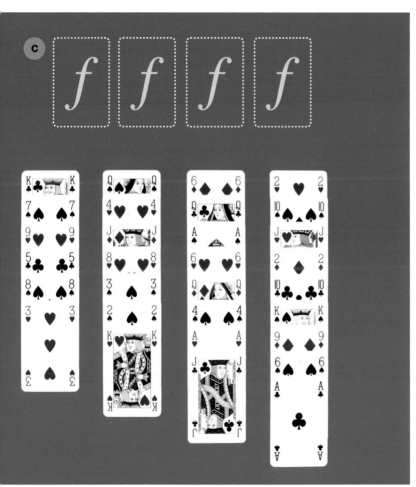

◄ Example of an initial layout

ⓐ Reserve
ⓑ Nine columns
ⓒ Foundation card spaces

● The final layout should consist of nine columns of face-up cards. The first column should have one card, the second two cards and so on up to the ninth column which has nine cards. Only the bottom card of each row is fully exposed.

● The remaining seven cards are laid out in a spread, or held in the hand, and form the reserve. Space is needed for the four Aces, which serve as foundations when they are freed for play.

Playing

● The cards in the reserve and the exposed cards from each column are available for play.

● If an Ace is available for play, it should be placed above the columns to act as the foundation card for its suit. A card that is available for play may be placed on a foundation Ace of the same suit if that available card continues the Ace-to-King ranking sequence. A card may also be played onto any other exposed card in a column if that exposed card is of the opposite colour and ranks immediately above the card to be played. For example, an available seven of clubs (black) may only be played to an exposed eight of hearts (red) or diamonds (red).

● Descending sequences of alternating colour may be moved to exposed cards in other columns. If a column is empty, it may be occupied by any available card from another column or by any descending sequence in another column if the last card of that sequence is available for play.

● Play continues in this way until no further moves can be made, or until all four Aces have been released and ranking sequences up to Kings of the same suit have been built on them.

EXAMPLE OF PLAY

Example of possible play for the layout on the previous pages:

1 The A♣ (exposed at the bottom of the ninth column) and the A♦ (from the reserve) should immediately be placed in two of the spaces for foundation cards. The 6♠ is now exposed in the ninth column.

2 The 2♣ (the card in the first column) and the 3♣ (exposed at the bottom of fifth column) can be placed, in turn, on the A♣ foundation. The 5♦ is now exposed in the fifth column and the first column is empty.

3 The J♣ (exposed at the bottom of the eighth column) may be moved into the empty first column, leaving the A♥ exposed in the eighth column so that it can be moved into a foundation card space.

Klondike

Klondike is one of the most popular patience games. It is also, perhaps surprisingly, one of the hardest to complete. Winning requires a pleasing balance of skill and sheer luck. The game is also known in Britain as Canfield.

Objective

To release the Aces to act as foundation cards and then to build consecutive sequences in the same suits.

Card values

Klondike is played with a single, standard deck of 52 cards. The cards rank in their suits with Kings highest, followed by Queens, Jacks, tens, nines, eights, sevens, sixes, fives, fours, threes, twos and Aces (lowest).

Layout

● Seven cards are dealt in a row, the first face-up and the next six face-down. Six cards are then dealt, the first face-up on the second card of the first row, and the next face-down on the next five cards of the first row. Successive rows of five, four, three, two and one card are dealt to each row beginning with a face-up card on the pile immediately to the right of the pile on which the previous row was started.

● The final layout should consist of seven columns of cards, each one with one more card than the last and with the top card face-up. The remainder of the pack is kept face-down as the stock. Space is needed above the rows of cards for the four foundation Aces when they become available and another space is needed for a discard pile.

Playing

● The top card turned over from the stock and the exposed face-up cards from the end of the columns are available for play. If the top card from the stock is not playable, it must be placed, face-up, on the discard pile. The top card of the discard pile is also always available for play.

● If an Ace is available for play, it should be placed above the columns to act as the foundation card for its suit. A card that is available for play may be placed on a foundation Ace of the same suit if that available card continues the Ace-to-King ranking sequence. A card may also be played onto any other exposed card in a column if that exposed card is of the

▶ Example
of an initial
layout

ⓐ Seven
columns
ⓑ Discard
pile space
ⓒ Foundation
card spaces

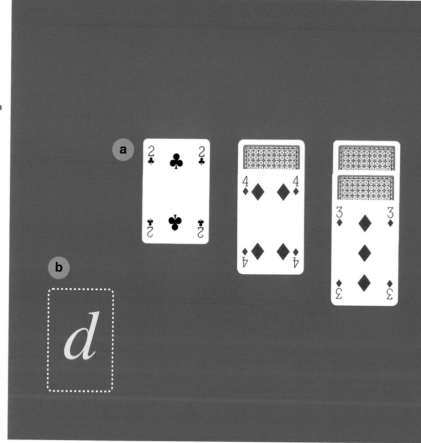

opposite colour and ranks immediately above the card to be played. For example, an available seven of clubs (black) may only be played to an exposed eight of hearts (red) or diamonds (red). When a card is played from a column, the next card in that column is turned face-up and becomes available for play.

● Descending sequences of alternating colour that are already face-up may be moved to exposed cards in other columns. If a column is empty, it may only be occupied by an available King. Kings may be moved into an unoccupied column along with any face-up cards that have already been built on it in the same descending ranking order of alternating colours.

● Play continues in this way until no further moves can be made, or until all four Aces have been released and ranking sequences up to Kings of the same suit have been built on them.

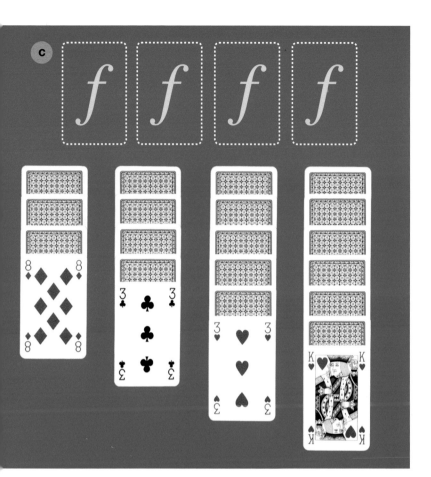

EXAMPLE OF PLAY

Example of possible play for the layout on this page:

1 The first card turned up from the stock is 10♣. This card cannot be played to any exposed card so it is placed face-up on the discard pile.
2 The exposed card in the first column, 2♣, may be built on the 3♦ (ranks immediately above 2 and is the opposite colour) in the third column. The first column is now empty.
3 The exposed K♥ in the seventh column may be placed in the empty first column (only Kings may be placed in empty columns). The last card in the seventh column is turned face up. It is A♦.
4 The A♦ is placed in one of the foundation spaces and the next card in the column is turned face-up.

Knights

Knights is a simple patience game in which the Jacks from each suit take part in an epic struggle to win points against each other. The game is also known as Contending knights.

Objective

To distribute even-numbered cards to the red Jacks and odd-numbered cards to the black Jacks and then to determine a 'winning' Jack.

Card values

Knights is played with a single, standard deck of 52 cards. All cards have the same rank. The Jacks are used to denote four 'teams': two red (hearts and diamonds) and two black (spades and clubs).

Layout

The four Jacks are laid out in a row with the Jack of hearts first, the Jack of clubs second, the Jack of diamonds third and the Jack of spades last. Space is needed under the row of Jacks for columns of cards that are formed during play. The remainder of the pack forms a face-down stock.

► Example of the initial layout

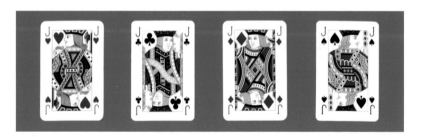

Playing

● Four cards from the stock are dealt face-up on the table. Any of the cards that are even-numbered are placed beneath the Jack of hearts; any of those cards that are odd-numbered are placed beneath the Jack of clubs. Kings are counted as even-numbered and Queens as odd-numbered.

● Four more cards are dealt but this time even-numbered cards are placed beneath the Jack of diamonds and odd-numbered cards beneath the Jack of spades. The process continues with successive four-card deals until the entire stock has been dealt and allocated.

- If all four cards in a deal are even-numbered or odd-numbered, they are allocated to the appropriate Jack, but that Jack also receives one card from each of the other Jacks, if they have any to give.
- When the stock has been exhausted, the total number of cards captured by each Jack is counted. Any Jack that has captured more than twelve cards receives one point for each card in excess of twelve.
- The cards (apart from the Jacks) are collected and reshuffled and the same four-card dealing sequence is repeated until the stock is exhausted for the second time. The cards are shuffled again and the process repeated for a third and final time. The Jack that has amassed the most points at the end of the three rounds wins the game.
- The game can be made more interesting by allowing other players to bet on which Jack will win. The whole game could also be used as an elaborate method of choosing a dealer for a subsequent four-player game with each player being appointed a Jack as his representative.

◀ Example of a layout during play

Queen's audience

NUMBER
OF CARDS

52

One deck
of 52 cards

Queen's audience is a simple patience game with an elegant layout. It has rather unusual rules and a fairly high chance of getting all the cards out.

Objective

To build suits on Jacks (the foundation cards) in descending rank order.

Card values

RANKING
ORDER

high

low

Queen's audience is played with a single, standard deck of 52 cards. The cards rank in their suits with Aces highest, followed by Kings, Queens, Jacks, tens, nines, eights, sevens, sixes, fives, fours, threes and twos (lowest).

Layout

- Sixteen cards are dealt, face-up, to form a square with four cards along each side. These sixteen cards are known as the 'Queen's antechamber'. The space enclosed by these sixteen cards is known as the 'Queen's audience chamber'.
- The four Jacks are placed in a row inside the audience chamber as they become available. The Kings and Queens go to form a separate pile inside the audience chamber as they become available.
- The remaining cards are placed face-down as a stock pile.
- Space is needed for a discard pile outside the audience chamber.

Playing

- The top card of the stock pile and all the cards in the antechamber are initially available to play.
- Jacks and Aces of the same suit should be placed, face-up, to form a foundation for that suit (the Jack should be uppermost).
- Kings and Queens of the same suit should be placed, also face-up, in the top left corner of the audience chamber (the Queen should be uppermost). This is known as the 'Royal discard pile'.
- Jacks can only be moved to form foundations if the Ace of the same suit is available for play. Similarly, Queens may only be moved if the King of the same suit is available.
- Unplayable cards from the stock must be placed face-up on the discard pile outside the audience chamber.

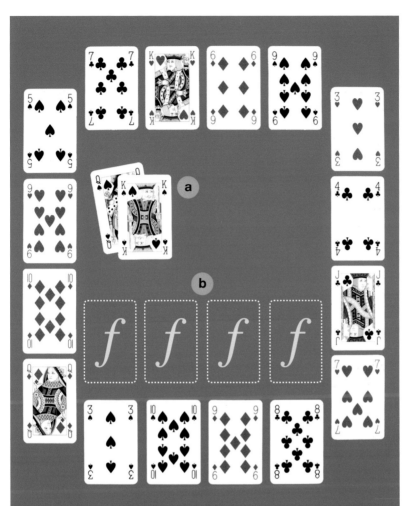

ⓐ Royal discard pile ⓑ Foundation card spaces

● The top card of the stock pile, the top card of the discard pile and any card in the antechamber is available for building descending sequences of rank on any Jacks that have been moved into their positions as foundation cards.

● Gaps in the antechamber must be filled with the top card of the discard pile, or with the next card from the stock if the discard pile is empty.

● Play continues in this way until the stock and the discard piles have been exhausted and all the cards in the antechamber have been built onto the appropriate sequence or the royal discard pile.

Siege

NUMBER
OF CARDS

52

One deck
of 52 cards

Siege is a classic patience game of moderate difficulty. It is also known as Beleaguered castle and gets its name from its layout, which resembles a fortress of Aces besieged by columns of troops.

Objective

To build suits on Aces (the foundation cards) in ascending rank order.

Card values

RANKING
ORDER

high

low

Siege is played with a single, standard deck of 52 cards. The cards rank in their suits with Kings highest, followed by, Queens, Jacks, tens, nines, eights, sevens, sixes, fives, fours, threes, twos and Aces (lowest).

Layout

The four Aces are laid out, in any order, in a face-up column. One card is then dealt, face-up, to the right and to the left of each Ace from top to bottom. A second card is then dealt to the right and left in each Ace in the same order so that the first card is still visible. Dealing continues in this way until each Ace has a column of six cards on its left and its right, with the last card in each column exposed. All the cards are dealt.

Playing

● The exposed cards at the end of each column are available for play. A card may be played to the Ace-foundation of the same suit if it is the next card required in the sequence of ascending rank order. For example, an exposed two of clubs may be built on the Ace of clubs and, subsequently, an exposed three of clubs may be built on the two.

● A card may also be built on any other exposed card if the card to be played is of immediately preceding rank to the exposed card, irrespective of suit. For example, an exposed three of clubs may be built on an exposed four of hearts, diamonds, spades or clubs.

● If a column has no cards left, an exposed card from another column, or a sequential sequence from the end of another column may be moved into that space to start a new column. For example, an exposed three and a four preceding it in the same column may be moved.

● The game ends when no more moves can be made, or when the four ranking sequences of Ace to King have been completed.

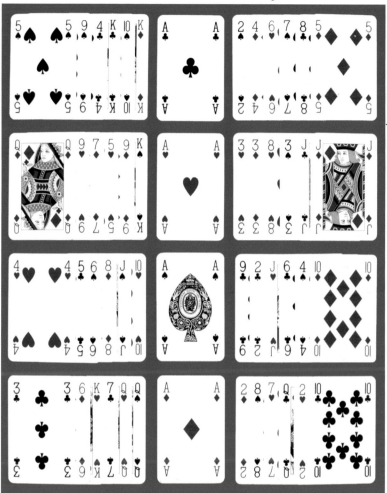

Left-hand columns   Foundation cards   Right-hand columns

◀ Example
of an initial
layout

EXAMPLE OF PLAY

Example of possible play for the layout above:

1 The 10♣ (exposed card in the bottom right column) can be built on the J♦ (exposed card in the column to the right of the A♥) to leave the 2♥ exposed.

2 The 2♥ can now be built on the A♥ foundation, leaving the Q♣ exposed.

3 The 2♦, 2♠ and 2♣ are buried deep within their columns. Cards preceding them in their columns will have to be built onto other columns before they can be released to play and the sequences continued.

games

for two

There are more card games for two players than for any other combination. Friends, partners and lovers have always enjoyed the challenge of a straightforward battle of wits that a round of Gin rummy or Bezique provides.

▶ All fives

NUMBER
OF CARDS

52

One deck
of 52 cards

All fives is a fairly simple trick-taking game for two players that is very similar to Seven up. It is essentially a variant of an older game called All fours that originated in England in the seventeenth century. All fours became popular in the United States and is also well known in the Caribbean today.

Objective

Players attempt to win tricks containing cards that are worth points.

RANKING
ORDER

high

low

Card values

All fives is played with a standard deck of 52 cards. Suits are ranked with Ace highest, followed by King, Queen, Jack, ten, nine, eight, seven, six, five, four, three and two (lowest).

Dealing

The first dealer is chosen at random or by mutual consent. Players take it in turns to deal throughout the game. Both players are dealt six cards, face-down, in two packets of three. The next card is dealt face-up to the centre of the table and is known as the 'upcard'.

Determining trumps

- The upcard is the basis for determining trumps. The dealer's opponent may decide to accept the suit of the upcard as the trump suit for that deal by calling 'stand', at which point trick-taking play begins. If the dealer's opponent does not want to accept the suit of the upcard as trumps, he should call 'I beg'.
- If the dealer's opponent calls 'I beg' the dealer may decide to keep the suit of the upcard as trumps by calling 'take one' which entitles the opponent to one point and allows trick-taking play to begin with the suit of the upcard as trumps.
- If the dealer's opponent calls 'I beg' and the dealer does not want to keep the suit of the upcard as trumps, he puts the upcard aside, deals three more cards to both players and then deals the next card as a new upcard. If the suit of the new upcard is different from the suit of the original upcard, trick-taking play begins with that suit as trumps. If the suit of the new upcard is the same as the suit of the original upcard, another three cards are dealt to each player plus another upcard. This process

continues until an upcard with a suit different to the original upcard is dealt. That suit becomes the trump suit for the deal and trick-taking play begins. If the deck is exhausted before a suitable upcard is dealt, the cards are passed to the dealer's opponent to be reshuffled and redealt.

Playing

- If an extended deal takes place in order to determine the trump suit, players must discard all but six cards from their hands. Any cards may be discarded.
- Play begins with the dealer's opponent and then passes alternately from player to player. The player who begins is said to 'lead' the trick. To lead, a player places one card face-up in the centre of the table. The suit of this card is the 'lead' suit of the trick.
- The next player must play a card of the same suit as the lead suit if he has one. If he has no card of the lead suit, he may play any other card, including trump cards.
- The trick is won by the highest-ranking card of the lead suit if no trump card is played, or by the highest-ranking trump card (unless the lead suit and the trump suit are the same). A player who wins a trick leads the next trick. Play continues until six tricks have been played, at which point the players will have no more cards.

EXAMPLES OF PLAY

Examples of possible trick-taking play involving trumps (clubs):

| Trick 1 | Trick 2 | Trick 3 |

Trick 1   The trick is lead by 3♣. Clubs are the lead suit and the trump suit. The second player has clubs and so must follow suit. He plays 4♣, which ranks higher than the lead card, and wins the trick.

Trick 2   The trick is lead by 10♠. The second player has no spades and plays 5♣, which wins the trick because it is a trump card.

Trick 3   The trick is lead by 10♣. The second player has no clubs and plays 3♦. 10♣ wins the trick because it is a trump card.

EXAMPLES OF PLAY

Examples of possible trick-taking play not involving trumps:

| Trick 1 | Trick 2 | Trick 3 |

Trick 1 The trick is lead by 8♣ so clubs are the lead suit. The second player has no clubs and chooses to play 5♠ (he could have played a trump card, if he had one, and won the trick). 8♣ wins the trick because it is the highest-ranking card of the lead suit.

Trick 2 The trick is lead by 8♥. The second player has hearts and so must follow suit. He plays J♥, which wins the trick because it is the highest-ranking card of the lead suit.

Trick 3 The trick is lead by 9♦. The second player has diamonds and so must follow suit. He plays Q♦, which wins the trick because it is the highest-ranking card of the lead suit.

Scoring

● Once all six tricks have been played, points are scored by each player depending on the cards contained in the tricks that they have won. Points are only awarded for tricks containing certain trump cards as shown in the table below:

POINT VALUES FOR CARDS

Trump card	Points
Ace	4
King	3
Queen	2
Jack	1
Ten	10
Five	5

● The game is won by the first player to reach 61 points. In the case of a tie, the player who reached 61 points first, according to the order in which tricks were taken, wins the game.

ALL FIVES

Strategy tips

- As in most trick-taking games, deciding when to accept a suit as trumps and when to reject it is of critical importance. The dealer's opponent should only accept the suit of an initial upcard as trumps if he is reasonably sure that he can win the majority of the ensuing tricks with the cards he has been dealt. This inevitably means that more than half of the cards he is holding must be in that suit.
- When discarding cards after an extended deal, a player should attempt to retain cards that make up a consecutive run in the same suit, even if that suit is not the trump suit. Playing these cards will tend to exhaust cards of the same suit from an opponent's hand.

All fives variants

▶ **THREE-HANDED ALL FIVES**

- All fives is often played as a three-player game. The rules are the same as two-handed All fives except that the dealership passes in a clockwise direction around the table rather than alternating between the two players.
- When determining trumps in a three-handed game, the player to the dealer's left has the opportunity to call 'stand' or 'I beg', and the third player is not involved in determining trumps until the next deal when he will be the player to the new dealer's left. Play to the first trick also begins with the player to the dealer's left and proceeds clockwise.

▶ **PENALTIES**

- Some players include penalty points in All fives games. A penalty of three points is incurred by any player who does not follow the lead suit when he is able to. This is known as a 'revoke'.
- A revoke must be called by an opponent after a trick has ended but before the next trick is lead.
- A player guilty of a revoke may not win a trick even if he played a winning card. Instead, the trick is awarded to his opponent in a two-handed game or to the player of the second-highest-ranking card in a three-handed game.
- If a player allows one of his cards to be seen face-up other than during the normal course of play, he must leave that card face-up on the table until an opponent requires him to play it to a trick by saying 'call'. A call may not be made if it will cause a revoke.

Bezique

Bezique originated in France where it evolved from similar
games played in the early seventeenth century. Bezique
became very popular in Britain during the nineteenth century
and gave rise to a number of variants. Bezique is regarded
as the forerunner of the popular US game Pinochle.

Objective

Players attempt to create point-winning melds and to win tricks that
contain point-winning cards.

Card values

- Bezique is played with two standard decks from which all of the twos,
threes, fours, fives and sixes have been removed. The two decks are
combined to make a playing deck of 64 cards.
- The cards in a suit rank with Ace highest, followed by the ten, King,
Queen, Jack, nine, eight and seven (lowest).

High   Low

▶ Card
ranking

Preparing

- Specialised Bezique scoring boards are available commercially.
Alternatively, a Cribbage scoring board may be used, or scores may
be recorded with pencil and paper.
- Players should also
agree whether the winning
score should be 1000 or
2000 points.

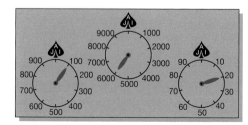

▶ Bezique
scoring board

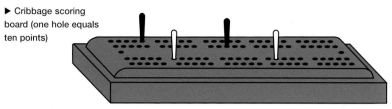

▶ Cribbage scoring board (one hole equals ten points)

Dealing

● The first dealer is chosen at random or by mutual consent and the dealership subsequently alternates between the players. The cards are shuffled by the dealer and cut by his opponent before the deal is made.

● Eight cards are dealt face-down to both players. A packet of three cards is dealt first, followed by a packet of two and then a second packet of three. The next card is dealt face-up to the centre of the table and is known as the 'upcard'. Remaining cards are left face-down next to the upcard to form the 'stock'.

● The suit of the upcard becomes the trump suit for the deal. If the upcard is a seven, the dealer immediately scores ten points.

Playing

Play takes place in two stages. Both involve trick-taking and making melds, but slightly different rules apply.

Stage one

● The dealer's opponent starts play for the first trick; he is said to 'lead' the trick. To lead, he places any card from his hand face-up in the centre of the table. The suit of that card is known as the 'lead' suit of the trick.

● The second player may play any card from his hand. The trick is won by the highest card played from the lead suit if no trump cards were played, or by the highest-ranking trump card. If both players play identical cards, the trick is won by the player who led. The second player is not compelled to play a card of the lead suit or a card of the trump suit: he may deliberately lose a trick if he chooses.

● The winner of the first trick checks his cards (including the cards won in the trick) to see if he can form any of the point-winning melds. The point-winning melds are shown in the table on the next page.

● A player may declare that he has one of the these melds by laying the relevant cards face-up in front of him and calling the name of the meld. For example 'Four Jacks' or 'Bezique'.

● Each of these melds is worth points, as shown in the table at the top of page 47.

▶ Point-winning melds with clubs as trumps

a Double bezique
Two Queens of spades and two Jacks of diamonds.
b Royal sequence
Ace, ten, King, Queen and Jack of the trump suit.
c Sequence
Ace, ten, King, Queen and Jack of the same suit.
d Four aces
One Ace from each suit.

e Four kings
One King from each suit.
f Four queens
One Queen from each suit.
g Four Jacks
One Jack from each suit.
h Bezique
Queen of spades and Jack of diamonds.
i Double royal marriage
Two trump Kings and Queens.

j Royal marriage
Trump King and Queen.
k Double common marriage
Two Kings and two Queens from the same suit.
l Common marriage
King and Queen from the same suit.
m Seven
Seven of the trump suit (exchanged for the upcard).

MELD POINT VALUES

Meld	Points	Meld	Points
Double bezique	500	Bezique	40
Royal sequence	250	Double royal marriage	40
Sequence	100	Royal marriage	40
Four Aces	100	Double common marriage	20
Four Kings	80	Common marriage	20
Four Queens	60	Seven	10
Four Jacks	40		

• Cards that have been used to form part of a meld can be used to declare subsequent melds if all of the cards needed for that subsequent meld were in the original meld. For example, the cards of a Royal sequence (Ace, ten, King, Queen and Jack of trumps) may be used to declare a subsequent meld of Royal marriage (King and Queen of trumps) since all of the cards needed to declare a Royal marriage were in the original Royal sequence.

• Cards that have been used to form part of a meld may not be used to form other melds of the same kind. For example, a Queen of diamonds used to form a Common marriage with a King of diamonds cannot subsequently be used to form a second Common marriage with another King of diamonds. The same Queen could, however, be used with its original partner in a subsequent declaration of Double marriage (because that is a meld of a different kind) if the player found himself holding a second Queen and King of diamonds.

• Cards that have been used to form part of a meld can also be used to declare subsequent melds with cards that a player captures in later tricks. For example, a Queen of diamonds that has already been used in a meld may subsequently be melded with Queens from the other three suits for a declaration of Four Queens. Three of the Queens in that declaration could not, however, subsequently be melded with a fifth Queen to form a second Four-Queens declaration: four new Queens would be needed for a player to make such a declaration.

• If a player declares a meld and uses one or more cards from his hand, he draws a card from the stock and adds it to his hand. Cards that are face-up as part of a meld may be played to subsequent tricks.

• A player who holds the seven of trumps may exchange it for the upcard, which counts as a declaration. A player who holds the second seven of trumps may also declare it for points but does not receive a card if the upcard has already been exchanged.

● Play continues in this manner until a player takes the last stock card. His opponent takes the upcard (which will either be the original upcard, or the seven of the same suit).

Stage two

● The winner of the last trick in stage one leads the first trick in stage two. Eight more tricks are played, one for each of the cards in a hand. In this stage a player must follow the lead suit if he is able and must play a card of the lead suit that will win the trick if he has one. If a player has no cards of the lead suit, he must play a trump that will win the suit if he has one. A player may play any other card, only if he is not able to play a card that would win a trick. No declarations are made in the second stage.

● The player who wins the last trick gains ten points. Players then check the cards they have captured for tricks that contain tens or Aces. A captured trick containing a ten or an Ace is known as a 'Brisque'. Each captured Brisque adds ten points to the player's total.

MUST KNOW

Strategy tips
● If you hold the seven of trumps and the upcard is higher than a nine (therefore a ten or greater of trumps), it is a good idea to declare it and exchange for that card as soon as possible.
● It is vital to keep on eye on the cards that an opponent plays and declares. There is little point in aiming to collect cards for a declaration of, for example, Double bezique, if your opponent has already played one of the Jack of diamonds.
● Be aware of any cards in your own hand that your opponent would like to collect. As long as you do not reveal that you hold a particular card by displaying it in a declared meld, your opponent may continue to collect cards for a meld that he cannot finish without that card. For example, if you hold a Queen of spades and an opponent has revealed that he has both Jacks of diamonds by declaring a Bezique with one and Four Jacks with the other, it is a good idea to keep your Queen concealed in the hope that the opponent will go on expecting it will turn up from the stock and allow him to declare a Double bezique as well.
● Great care is needed in the second stage. Always lead the first tricks with Aces or tens if you are sure an opponent has at least one lower value card of

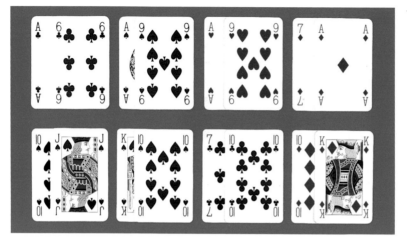

● The first player to reach 1000 or 2000 points (depending on the winning total agreed before play began) wins the game. In the case of a tie, the player that reached the winning total first, according to the order in which tricks were taken in the second stage, wins the game.

▼ A 17th-century French Queen of hearts

the same suit. Never lose sight of the fact that the number of Brisques you win is more important than the sheer number of tricks. You will not gain any points by winning seven of the eight tricks if none of them contains trumps. Therefore, any trump cards that you hold should be played very carefully to ensure that you retain possession of them. If at all possible, only play trump cards when you are sure they will win the trick. It would be very unwise to lead the first trick of the second stage with your highest-value trump since your opponent may be able to beat it.

● An opponent is very likely to use his highest-value trump in the final trick of the second stage to secure the extra ten points. Do not waste your own highest trump by keeping it for the last trick unless you are sure that your opponent does not have a higher trump. Suppose, for example, that you keep the ten of trumps to lead the last trick and your opponent has the Ace of trumps. Your opponent will win not only the extra ten points for the last trick (which is unavoidable in this situation), he will also hold a Brisque that could have been yours if you had used your ten of trumps in a previous trick.

BEZIQUE

49

Bezique variants

▶ **RUBICON BEZIQUE**
● Rubicon bezique is an extended version of Bezique that uses a deck with more cards and includes extra declarations.

Cards and dealing
● All cards below the value of seven (not including Aces) are removed from four standard decks and the remainder are combined to make a playing deck of 128 cards.
● Players receive nine cards each in three packets of three. No upcard is dealt. Trumps are determined by the suit of the first marriage or sequence to be declared by either player.

Melds
● There are four additional melds that may be declared:

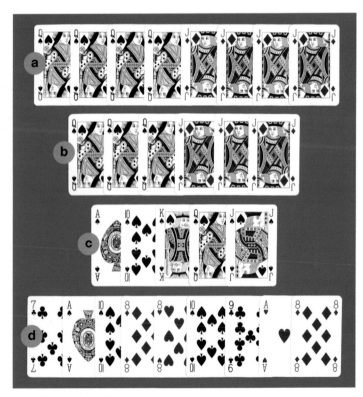

▲ Additional melds in Rubicon bezique

ⓐ Quadruple bezique
Four Queens of spades and four Jacks of diamonds.
Worth 4500 points.

ⓑ Triple bezique
Three Queens of spades and three Jacks of diamonds.
Worth 1500 points.

ⓒ Back door or Ordinary sequence
Ace, ten, King, Queen and Jack of a non-trump suit.
Worth 150 points.

▼ A 17th-century six of hearts

ⓓ Carte blanche
Declared by a player who has been dealt a hand
without court cards. The hand is displayed and the
player draws a card from the stock. If this card is
not a court card, Carte blanche may be declared
again. The process continues until the player draws
a court card. Worth 50 points per declaration.

● Cards used in declared melds may be used in
subsequent similar melds. For example, if a Four
Queen meld has been declared and the player
draws another Queen, he may declare a second
Four Queen meld using the new Queen plus three
of the Queens in the original meld.

Playing
● Rules for playing are the same as for standard
Bezique, except that winning the last trick of the second stage is
worth 50 points.

Scoring
● If the loser of a deal earns less than 1000 points, he is said to
be 'rubiconed'.
● In the event of a rubicon the winner receives an additional 1000
points plus the sum of both player's scores plus 320 points regardless
of whether his own basic score is more or less than 1000 points.
● If there is no rubicon, the winner receives 500 points plus the
difference between his own and the loser's score.
● Brisques are not normally counted unless a player is close to being
rubiconed or in the event of a tie.
● The game is won by the player with the highest cumulative score
at the end of the number of deals that has been agreed in advance.

Bezique variants continued...

▶ **CHINESE BEZIQUE**
- Chinese bezique is another extended version of Bezique that uses a deck with more cards and some extra meld declarations.

Cards and dealing
- All cards below the value of seven (not including Aces) are removed from six standard decks and the remainder are combined to make a playing deck of 192 cards.
- Players receive twelve cards each in four packets of three. No upcard is dealt. Trumps are determined by the suit of the first Marriage or Sequence to be declared by either player.

Melds
- There are five additional melds that may be declared:

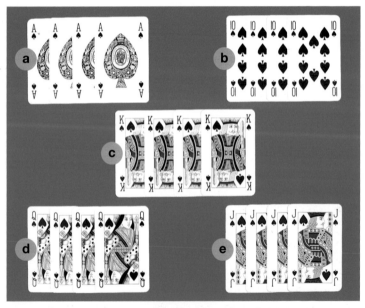

▲ Additional melds in Chinese bezique with spades as trumps

- **ⓐ** Four trump Aces. Worth 1000 points.
- **ⓑ** Four trump Tens. Worth 900 points.
- **ⓒ** Four trump Kings. Worth 800 points.
- **ⓓ** Four trump Queens. Worth 600 points.
- **ⓔ** Four trump Jacks. Worth 400 points.

- Declarations of Bezique vary according to which suit is trumps:

| Bezique with hearts as trumps | Bezique with diamonds as trumps | Bezique with clubs as trumps | Bezique with spades as trumps |

- Other melds and the rules of declaring are the same as for Rubicon bezique except that declarations of Carte blanche are worth 250 points each.

Playing
- Rules for playing are the same as for Rubicon bezique, except that winning the last trick of the second stage is worth 250 points.

Scoring
- Scoring is the same as for Rubicon bezique except that a winner whose opponent is rubiconed scores 3000 points, and a winner whose opponent is not rubiconed scores 1000 points. Brisques are never counted.

▶ **THREE-HANDED BEZIQUE**
- A variant of Bezique for three players.
- Players play individually.

Cards and dealing
- All cards below the value of seven (not including Aces) are removed from three standard decks and the remainder are combined to make a playing deck of 96 cards.
- All other aspects of dealing are the same as in standard Bezique.

Scoring
- Scores are tripled where opportunities arise for triple versions of the standard Bezique scoring combinations. For example, a triple Bezique earns 1500 points.
- The winning total is usually 3000 points.

Casino

Casino is an unusual card game in that it is the only 'fishing' game to have become popular in the English-speaking world. Fishing games are those in which players 'capture' cards in the layout using the cards that they hold.

Objective

To capture as many cards from the layout as possible.

Card values

Casino is played with a standard deck of 52 cards. Suits are ranked with the King highest, followed by Queen, Jack, ten, nine, eight, seven, six, five, four, three, two and Ace (lowest).

Dealing

The first dealer is chosen at random, or by mutual consent. Four cards are dealt, face-down, to each player and four cards are dealt, face-up, for the layout. Traditionally the cards are dealt in pairs.

Playing

Play begins with the player to the dealer's left and passes counterclockwise. A player may capture, build or trail.

Capturing

Capturing cards is the main aim of the game. Captured cards are worth points. There are four possible capturing manoeuvres: pair capture, group capture, group and pair capture, and court-card capture.

Pair capture

● A player may capture a card in the layout with a card in the hand that has the same face value.

● One, two or three cards in the layout may be captured at the same time if they all have the same face value (for example, a player holding 5♥ may capture 5♦, or 5♣, or 5♠, or two or all three of them if they happen to be in the layout).

● To capture a card a player places a card from the hand face-down onto the matching card and withdraws it from the layout. Each player's captured cards are kept in a face-down pile.

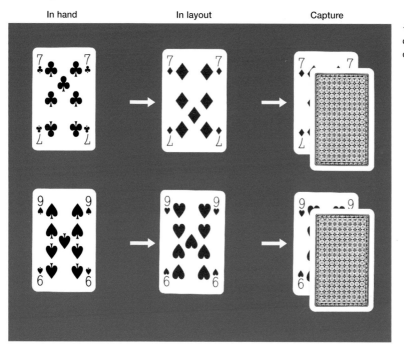

In hand   In layout   Capture

◄ Example of pair capture

Group capture

● A player may capture two or more cards with face values totalling the face value of a card in the hand.

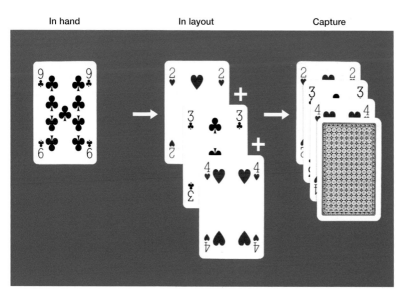

In hand   In layout   Capture

◄ Example of group capture

Group and pair capture

● A player may capture a group of two or more cards with face values totalling the face value of a card in the hand, plus a single card with the same face value.

● Capturing all the cards in the layout in the same turn is known as a 'sweep'. When a sweep occurs the next player is forced to trail (see Trailing, page 60).

▶ Example of a group and pair capture

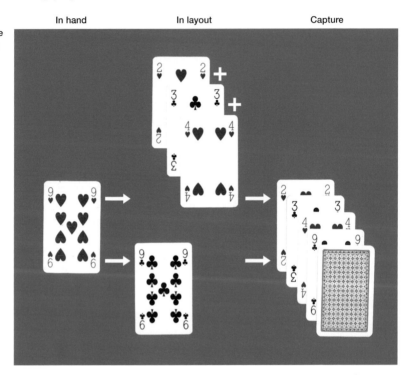

Court-card capture

● Court cards (the court cards are the King, the Queen and the Jack) are not used to capture in the same way as other cards.

● A player may use a court card to capture one matching face-up court card from the layout, or alternatively three matching face-up court cards from the layout if he holds the fourth.

● This means that if, for example, a player holds a Queen and there are two face-up Queens in the layout he can only capture one of them in a turn (he may capture either). If, on the other hand, a player holds a Queen and there are three face-up Queens in the layout, he may capture all three of them in the same turn.

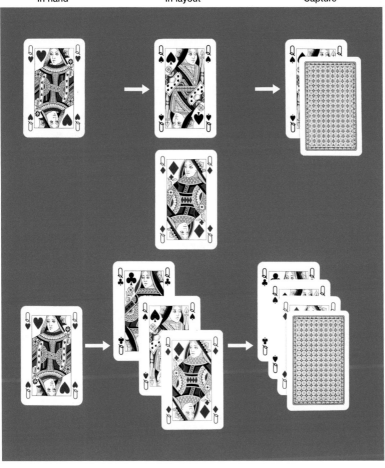

In hand	In layout	Capture

Building

Cards in the layout may be added to with cards from the hand. This is
known as building. The purpose of building is to increase the number of
cards that can be captured in the next turn.

Single build

● A player may make a single build by adding a card from the hand,
face-up, to a card in the layout provided that:

    a) the face values of the two cards added together is not more
than ten,

    b) the player making the build holds a card with a face value equal
to the value of the built cards added together.

- A player making a build must declare the value of the build (for example, a player holding a 7 and a 4 may build the 4 onto a 3 in the layout and declare 'building seven').

▶ Example of a single build (building seven)

In hand   In layout

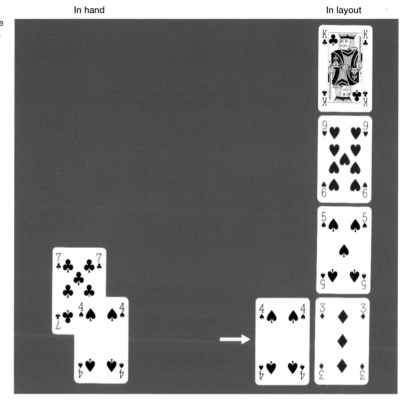

- A player may capture the cards contained in a build made by a previous player using a card in the hand with the same face value as the declared value of the build.
- A player may add to an existing build. For example, following the build illustrated above, a player holding a 2 and a 9 may build the 2 onto the built 7 in the layout and declare 'building nine'.
- Building can continue in this style until a player captures the built cards or until no more builds can be made without exceeding a built value of 10 (the maximum allowed).

Multiple build

- A multiple build consists of increasing the value of an existing build and adding a second build of the same value to the layout.

This is an example of a possible multiple build for the layout below:

1 A build of 5 has already been made (4♠ has been built on A♣).
2 The next player holds 5♣, 4♥, 4♦, and 9♣.
3 The 4♥ is built on the existing build of 5 to create a build of 9. The 5♣ and the 4♦ are placed next to the new build to create a second build of the same value (9).
4 On the next turn, the player may use the 9♣ to capture A♣, 4♠, 4♥, 5♣ and 4♦.

In hand   In layout

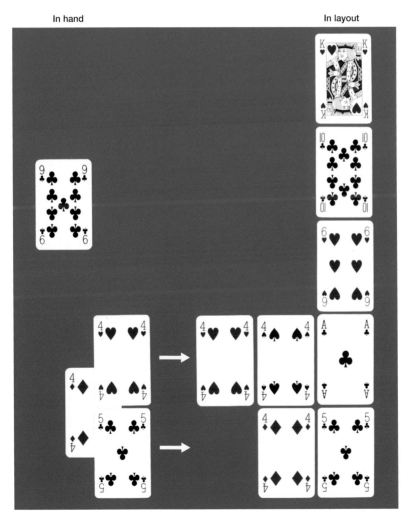

◀ Example of a multiple build (building nine)

Trailing

● Any player who cannot capture or build must 'trail'. Trailing means placing a card from the hand face-up on one end of the existing layout.

● Trailed cards becomes available for capture. This is the only time that cards are added to the basic layout.

● A player may trail as a matter of choice; he is not compelled to make a capture or a build, even if one is possible.

Replenishing cards

● New cards are dealt only when all players have used all four cards they were initially given. Players are then dealt another four cards, again, usually in pairs.

● After the initial deal, new cards are never dealt to the layout. The only new cards in the layout come from players trailing.

● Play continues until there are no cards left in the stock, at which point the round ends and scores are calculated.

Scoring

● At the end of a round players are awarded points for their captured cards according to the table below.

● Cards left in the layout after all players have played their cards, and none remain to be dealt from the stock, are awarded to the last player to have made a capture. The values of these cards contribute to that player's final score.

● Traditionally, rounds continue to be played until one player accumulates 21 points or more. If two players reach 21 points in a round, the player with the most points in excess of 21 wins.

● In the event of a draw, another round is played as a decider.

▼ A 19th-century German card depicting a sultan

POINT VALUES FOR CARDS

Card	Points
2 of spades (Little casino)	1
10 of diamonds (Big casino)	2
Each Ace	1
Seven or more spades	1
27 or more cards	3
A sweep	1

Strategy tips

- Spotting building opportunities is vitally important. The more cards you can use from your hand to create builds, the more cards there are available for you to capture.
- Practise remembering which cards have already been played. If you hold an eight and know, for example, that three eights have already been played or captured, you have a much better chance of successfully building, and then capturing, an eight.
- Retaining court cards can be an advantage. If a court card is left in the layout towards the end of a round you have a better chance of making the last capture and securing extra points.

Casino variants

▶ **ROYAL CASINO**

- Court cards have face values and may be used to capture, but not build.

Card	Face value
Jacks	11
Queens	12
Kings	13

- Aces may be given a face value of 14 or remain as 1. Players must agree on one or other value before play begins.

▶ **DRAW CASINO**

- The first twelve cards are dealt, as in the standard rules, but players replenish their own hands by drawing from the stock.

▶ **SPADE CASINO**

- Rules are identical to the standard game, except that additional points are awarded for certain captured spades

Card	Points
Ace of spades	2
Jack of spades	2
Two of spades	2
Other spades	1

- The first player to reach 61 points wins the game.

Cribbage

Cribbage originated in Britain and is reputed to have been invented by the early seventeenth-century poet Sir John Suckling. It is certainly based on an earlier card game called Noddy. Five-card cribbage was the original form of the game, but today Six-card cribbage is more popular and is the version described here.

Objective

Players try to gain points from combinations of cards that occur during the game or in the hand.

Card values

Cribbage is played with a standard deck of 52 cards. Suits rank with the King highest, followed by Queen, Jack, ten, nine, eight, seven, six, five, four, three, two and Ace (lowest). Court cards have a face value of ten.

Preparing

● Scores can be kept with pencil and paper, but many players prefer to use a purpose-made Cribbage board. A Cribbage board consists of a solid rectangular block with a double row of 60 or 61 peg holes for each player. Each player also has two pegs, usually white for one player and black or red for the other, with which to record their score.

▶ A standard
Cribbage
board and
pegs

● A player records his first score by placing a peg in the appropriate hole on the outer line of holes (one hole equals one point). His second score is recorded by placing the second peg the appropriate number of holes beyond the first to show the cumulative total. The next score is marked by moving the first peg the appropriate distance beyond the second, and so on.

▼ Moving pegs on a Cribbage board to record cumulative scores

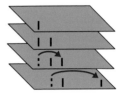

When a player reaches 31 points or more, he moves his pegs in the same manner, but in the opposite direction, along the inner line of holes. When he reaches 60 points (the end of the second row) the pegs are moved back along the first row again. Going twice around the double row, scoring 121 points, wins the game. Recording scores in this way means that the number of points scored in the last deal is always visible since it is shown by the distance between a player's two pegs.

Dealing

- The first dealer is chosen at random, or by mutual consent. Subsequently, the dealership alternates between the players. The dealer shuffles the deck and the non-dealer cuts the pack before the deal is made.
- Each player receives six cards, dealt face-down and one at a time. The remainder of the deck is placed face-down on the table.
- Both players discard any two cards, which are placed face-down on the table to form the 'Crib'. Any point-winning combinations of cards in the Crib will count towards the dealer's score at the end of the deal.
- The dealer's opponent cuts the cards in the undealt portion of the deck and turns the top card of the lower half of the cut face-up on the table. This is known as the 'start' card. If the start card is a Jack, the dealer gains two points (known as 'Two for his heels').

Playing

- The dealer's opponent starts play by placing one card from his hand face-up on the table and announcing its face value. For the purposes of this part of the game, cards are valued as shown in the table below:

FACE VALUES FOR CARDS

Card	Value
Court cards (King, Queen, Jack)	10
Ten – Ace	Index value (10 – 1)

- Players take it in turns to place one card at a time face-up on the table, keeping their own cards together. As each card is played, the player announces a running total of all the cards that have been put down. If this total reaches exactly 31, that player receives two points. If a player cannot put down another card without exceeding a total of 31 he calls 'go'.

● If a player calls 'go', his opponent may put down one more card. If that card brings the running total to exactly 31, he scores two points. If that card brings the total to less than 31, he scores one point for playing the last card. If he cannot put down a card without exceeding 31, or if he has no cards left, he too calls 'go'.

● Following a second call of 'go', all the cards on the table are turned face-down and the player who last called 'go' has the opportunity to start a new sequence, again aiming for an end total of 31. Play continues in this manner until both players have put down all their cards.

● During this stage of play, players receive points for any of the following combinations in their sequences:

▶ Point-scoring combinations

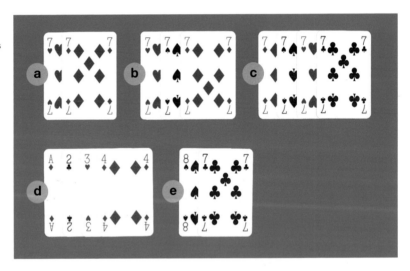

ⓐ Pair
A second card of the same rank earns two points. Note that court cards cannot be paired with tens, even though they have the same count value.

ⓑ Pair royal
A third card of the same rank after completing a Pair earns six points.

ⓒ Double pair royal
A fourth card of the same rank after completing a Pair royal earns twelve points.

ⓓ Run
Consecutive cards that make a sequence regardless of the suit of the cards. For example, 2♣, 3♦ and 4♠. The order in which the cards are played does not matter, as long as no other cards intervene. A Run earns the same number of points as there are cards in the Run.

ⓔ Fifteen
A card that brings the cumulative total to exactly 15 earns two points.

Scoring

● After the end of the sequence-playing phase, the dealer's opponent lays all his cards face-up on the table, along with the start card, (known as the 'Show') and scores them according to any of the following combinations that they contain:

POINT VALUES FOR COMBINATIONS

Combination held	Points
Fifteen Any combination of cards with face values totalling exactly fifteen, irrespective of suit	2
Pair Any pairs of cards of the same face value	2
Run Any three cards with consecutive face values, irrespective of suits	1 per card
Flush All four cards of the same suit*	4
One for his nob The Jack of the same suit as the start card	1

*A flush cannot be formed from three cards of the same suit plus a start card also of the same suit, but a five-card flush, worth five points, may be formed if all four cards from the hand are the same suit as the start card.

● The same cards may be used in as many different scoring combinations as possible.

● After the dealer's opponent has scored his cards, the dealer scores his cards in the same way. The Crib is then shown and scored in the same way, except that only five-card flushes are counted. The score from the Crib is added to the dealer's total.

● The first player to reach 121 points, or more, wins the game.

● A player may win the game at any stage, including during the deal if the dealer gains two points for turning up a Jack as the start card. As soon as a player reaches 121 points, the game ends and points that would have been scored by his opponent had play continued are not counted. For example, if the dealer's opponent reaches 121 points during the show, the dealer's cards and the Crib are not shown, even though they may have netted more points than the non-dealer's winning total.

EXAMPLE OF SCORING

The hand, plus the start card, shown below yield the scoring combinations shown:

1 The start card is 4♥. The player has 4♣, 5♥, 6♣ and 6♠ in his hand.
2 There are four possible combinations of the five cards that make a total of exactly fifteen. Each combination is worth two points, making a total of eight points for Fifteens.
3 The same four combinations are also runs of three cards. Each run is worth three points (since they each contain three cards) making a total of twelve points for Runs.
4 There are two pairs of cards with the same face value. Each pair is worth two points making a total of four points for Pairs.
5 There are no Flushes and no Jack to score. The player with this hand, in combination with this start card, scores a total of 24 points.

Start card   In hand

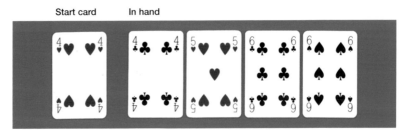

MUST KNOW

Strategy tips
● Discarding to the Crib is a critical stage of the game. If you are the dealer, the discard is much easier since you will have the benefit of any Point generated by the Crib. The dealer should put cards that are not benefiting his hand into the Crib. If there are no such cards, any five or two cards totalling five should be discarded. Any two cards totalling fifteen are also suitable candidates for discarding. The dealer's opponent should avoid discarding the same combinations, avoid discarding two cards with a gap of only one ranking between them (for example, a Queen and a ten) and avoid discarding two cards of the same suit.
● Always bear in mind that cards worth ten in the count outnumber any other card. It is therefore likely that your opponent will hold at least one and probably more than one. Avoid leading fives, which enable your opponent to make a point-winning count of fifteen with one of his tens, or making a total of

Fifteens

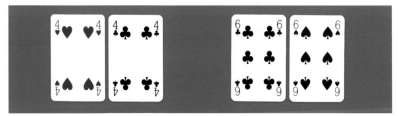

Pairs

21, which carries the risk of allowing your opponent to make a point-winning count of 31 for the same reason. This also means that making a count of eleven when you have a ten left in your hand is a good idea since there is a good chance it will force your opponent to make a count of 21.

● Playing a six to a led four, or a four to a led six, can be very risky. If your opponent holds a five he can play it to make a count of fifteen and a run of four, five and six.

● Higher-value cards should generally be played first, since they become more and more dangerous as the count approaches 31. Aces should be saved for as long as possible as they can turn a point-losing count of 30 into a point-winning total of 31.

● If you hold two cards that add up to five (for example an Ace and a four) lead the count with one of them. Your opponent is more likely than not to play a ten, which enables you to follow with the other and make a count of fifteen.

Cribbage variants

▶ **FIVE-CARD CRIBBAGE**
● Five-card cribbage is the original form of Cribbage. Although it has largely been supplanted by Six-card cribbage, it is still played throughout the world.

Cards and dealing
● The deck is the same as in Six-card cribbage. Players receive only five cards each. Two cards are still discarded to the Crib.
● For the first deal only, the dealer's opponent immediately receives three points as compensation for not having access to the Crib.

Playing
● During sequence-making play, only one sequence of 31 or less is made. As soon as one player completes a sequence of exactly 31, or when both players run out of cards, sequence play ends. It is possible for players to have unplayed cards at the end of this phase.

Scoring
● Point-winning combinations are the same as for Six-card cribbage. The game is won by the first player to reach 61 or more points. As in Six-card cribbage, the game ends when one player reaches the winning total.

▶ **SEVEN-CARD CRIBBAGE**
● All rules are the same as for Six-card cribbage, except that players are dealt seven cards and 181 points win the game.

▶ **THREE-HANDED CRIBBAGE**
● A variant of Six-card cribbage for three players.

Cards and dealing
● Each player receives five cards and contributes one to the Crib.

Playing
● The player to the left of the dealer begins sequence play and shows first. Sequences continue until all players have used all their cards.

Scoring
● The game is won by the first player to reach or exceed 61 points.

Ecarté

Ecarté became particularly popular in France in the nineteenth century and remains a popular game among French-speakers all over the world. Ecarté means 'discarded'. Euchre and Five hundred are both modern variants of Ecarté.

Objective
Players try to win points by taking more tricks than their opponents.

Card values
● Ecarté is played with a deck from which all sixes, fives, fours, threes and twos have been removed to create a playing deck of 32 cards.

● Cards in a suit rank with the King highest, followed by the Queen, Jack, Ace, ten, nine, eight and seven (lowest).

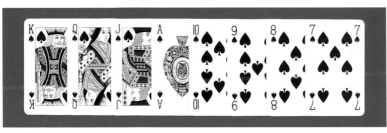

High   Low

◀ Card ranking

Dealing
● The first dealer is chosen at random, or by mutual consent, and the dealership subsequently alternates between the players. The dealer shuffles the cards and his opponent cuts them before the deal is made.

● Each player receives five cards dealt face-down in one packet of three cards followed by another packet of two cards. The next card is dealt face-up to the centre of the table and is known as the 'upcard'. The remainder of the deck is placed face-down next to the upcard to form the 'stock'.

● The suit of the upcard determines the trump suit for the duration of the deal.

● Once the deal has been made, the non-dealer may propose an exchange of cards by calling 'cards'. When an opponent calls 'cards' the dealer may allow the exchange by calling 'yes' or refuse by calling 'play'.

● If the dealer does not allow an exchange, play starts immediately.

● If the dealer allows an exchange, his opponent may discard as many cards as he wishes from his hand and replace them with cards drawn from the stock. The dealer may then do the same.

● Following an exchange, the non-dealer may call for a second exchange, which the dealer may allow or refuse in the same manner. The non-dealer may continue to call for exchanges until the dealer calls 'play'. If the stock is exhausted before the dealer calls 'play', the cards are reshuffled and passed to the dealer's opponent for a new deal.

▶ Card layout following a deal

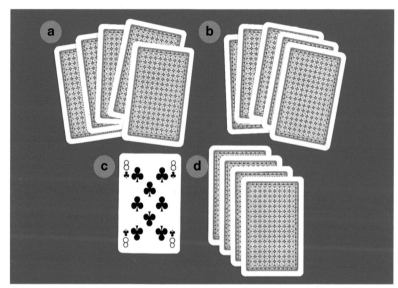

ⓐ Dealer's hand   ⓑ Non-dealer's hand   ⓒ Upcard (clubs are trumps)   ⓓ Stock

Playing

● Play begins with the dealer's opponent and alternates between the players. The non-dealer begins by laying any card from his hand face-up on the table. This is known as 'leading' the trick. The suit of the first player's card is known as the 'lead' suit for the trick.

● The dealer must play one card from his hand. He must play a card of the lead suit if he has one. If he has no cards of the lead suit he must play a trump card if he has one. If he has no cards of the lead suit and no trump cards he may play any other card.

● The trick is won by the highest-ranking card of the lead suit if no trumps were played, or by the highest-ranking trump.

● A player must win a trick if he has a card that will enable him to do so.

● The player who wins the trick leads the next trick.

Scoring

- Once all five tricks have been played, players score points according to the number of tricks they have won. Winning three tricks, known as 'Point' or the 'Trick', earns one point. Winning all five tricks, known as the 'Vole', earns two points.

- If the upcard is a King, the dealer immediately wins one point. If a player holds the King of the trump suit, he may declare it and earn one point as long as he declares before he plays his first card to a trick.

- The game is won by the first player to reach five points. In the case of a tie, another five tricks are played as a decider.

MUST KNOW

Strategy tips

- The only real strategic decision to be made in Ecarté is when to call for an exchange and when to prevent an exchange if you are the dealer. Certain hands should always be kept intact if possible by not calling 'cards' if you are the non-dealer, or by calling 'play' if you are the dealer. These hands are known as 'jeux de regle', and all have a high chance of beating any opposing hand:

    1) Any hand that contains three or more trumps.

    2) Any hand that contains two trumps and three other cards of the same suit.

    3) Any hand that contains two trumps and two other cards of the same suit that are at least as high-ranking as a Queen.

    4) Any hand that contains two trumps and three other cards from different suits that are Kings or Jacks.

    5) Any hand that contains a ranking sequence of four consecutive cards in the same suit with a King as the highest-ranking card.

    6) Any hand that contains two Kings and three other cards of the same suit.

Ecarté variants

▶ **CARD EXCHANGE**

- Some players call 'I propose' rather than 'cards' when playing as non-dealer and asking for a card exchange. The dealer's reply in this case should be 'play' to refuse the exchange or 'I accept' to allow it.

- Some players do not redeal in the situation where a succession of exchanges have exhausted the stock. Instead, players must play with the cards they hold at the point when the stock is exhausted.

Gin rummy

Gin rummy is a very popular variant of Rummy. Its main attractions are its simplicity and speed of play compared to its more involved parent. The game described here is sometimes also known as 500 Rummy.

Objective

Players aim to combine as many of their cards as possible into point-winning melds known as 'sequences' and 'groups'.

Card values

● Gin rummy is played with a single standard deck of 52 cards. The cards in a suit are ranked with the King highest, followed by the Queen, Jack, ten, nine, eight, seven, six, five, four, three, two and Ace (lowest).

High   Low

● Cards have values as shown in the table below:

FACE VALUES FOR CARDS

Card	Value
Court cards (King, Queen, Jack)	10
Ten – Ace	Index value (10 – 1)

Dealing

● The first dealer is chosen at random, or by mutual consent, and the dealership subsequently alternates between the players.

● Each player is dealt ten cards, face-down and one at a time. The next card is dealt face-up to form the start of the discard pile and the remainder of the deck is placed face-down beside it to form the stock.

Playing

● The dealer's opponent has the opportunity to add the one card in the discard pile to his hand. If he refuses the card, the dealer has the opportunity to add it to his hand. If the dealer also refuses the card, the dealer's opponent takes the top card from the stock pile and adds it to his hand. Whichever player added a card to his hand must then discard one card, face-up to the discard pile.

● For every subsequent turn, a player must pick up the top card from either the discard pile or the stock and end his turn by discarding a card from his hand to the discard pile. A player may not discard a card taken from the discard pile in the same turn.

● A player may 'knock' during any turn. To knock, a player raps on the table and lays any cards in his hand that form sets face-up on the table. There are two forms of sets: 'sequences' and 'groups'. A sequence consists of three or more consecutively-ranked cards in the same suit. A group consists of three or four cards of the same rank from different suits. A card may only be used in one set. A player may only knock if any cards from his hand not used in sets have a total value of ten or less.

◀ Sets

Group   Sequence

● A player may only knock after he has taken a card from the discard pile or the stock at the start of that turn. A player must discard a card after knocking to end his turn.

● A player who knocks and uses all of his cards to form sets is said to have 'gone gin'.

● When a player knocks without going gin, his opponent must immediately place all of his cards face-up on the table and form as many sets from them as possible. He may then use any unmatched cards to add to sets laid down by the player who knocked. When a player goes gin, his opponent must turn all his cards face-up and form as many sets as possible, but may not use any unmatched cards to add to the sets made by the player that knocked.

● A player is never compelled to knock.

- If no player has knocked by the time there are only two cards left in the stock, the hand is abandoned. The cards are reshuffled and a new deal is made by the original dealer.
- Play ends when one player knocks and his opponent has arranged his cards into sets.

Scoring

- Both players calculate the total value of any unmatched cards from their hands. If the value of the knocker's unmatched cards is less than the value of his opponent's unmatched cards, the knocker receives the same number of points as the difference between the two totals. If the value of the knocker's unmatched cards is greater than the value of his opponent's unmatched cards, he is said to be 'undercut' and his opponent receives ten points plus the same number of points as the difference between the two values.
- If a player goes gin, he receives twenty points plus the combined value of any unmatched cards in his opponent's hand. A player who goes gin can never be undercut. Even if his opponent has no unmatched cards, he still wins twenty points and his opponent wins nothing. When a player wins a deal, a line is drawn under or around his winning score.
- Deals continue until one player reaches 100 points or more. That player receives an additional 100 points, unless his opponent failed to score any points during the game, in which case the bonus is 200 points. Players then add twenty points to their totals for every deal they win. These are known as 'line' or 'box' bonuses.
- Once all bonuses have been allocated, the player with the highest score receives points equal to the difference between the two scores. The same number of points are subtracted from his opponent's score.

MUST KNOW

- Watching which cards your opponent picks up from the discard pile and which he discards can give you valuable information about what he is trying to collect. If you have a card or cards that you suspect your opponent is looking for to complete sets, it is a good idea to keep it in your hand and only discard it when you knock.
- If you suspect that your opponent already has two sets containing at least three cards but has not knocked, it is likely that he is trying to go gin. Unless you are close to going gin yourself, it is usually wise to knock as soon as possible, to prevent your opponent from receiving the gin bonus.

Gin rummy variants

▶ **FIRST-TURN VARIANT**
- In some Gin rummy games, the non-dealer is dealt eleven cards and no card is turned up to start the discard pile.
- The non-dealer begins play by discarding one of his cards. The dealer then has his first turn with the option of picking up his opponent's discard or a card from the stock.
- All other rules remain the same.

▶ **OKLAHOMA GIN**
- A slightly more complex variant of Gin rummy that includes a variable limit to the value of unmatched cards.

Dealing
- The deal is the same as for Gin rummy, except that the value of the card dealt to start the discard pile determines the maximum value of unmatched cards that a player may hold after knocking. For example, if the base card of the discard pile is a seven, no player may knock unless any cards that he does not use to form sets have a combined value of seven or less. If the base card of the discard pile is an Ace, players may only knock if they can go gin.

Scoring
- If the base card of the discard pile is a spade, the final scores for that deal (including bonuses) are doubled.
- A player who undercuts a knocker receives a box or line bonus for that game in addition to the undercut bonus.
- A player who goes gin receives two extra box or line bonuses for that deal. If the base card of the discard pile is a spade, a player who undercuts receives two box or line bonuses and a player who goes gin receives four box or line bonuses.
- The winning total is 150 points or more

▶ **FOUR-HANDED GIN RUMMY**
- Players form two teams of two players each.
- Players compete against one member of the opposite team in separate games. Opponents alternate for each deal.
- If both players on a team win, they receive the total of their combined points. If one wins, the player with the higher score wins points equal to the difference between the two winning scores for his team.

Kalabriasz

Kalabriasz is part of a large family of very similar games that originated in the low countries of northern Europe. The game is sometimes known as Klabberjass or Clobiosh or Klob. The national card game of the Netherlands, Klaverjas, is also closely related.

Objective

Players try to complete sequences, or melds, and win certain high-scoring cards by taking tricks.

Card values

● All cards with a face value below seven (except the Aces) are removed from a standard deck to leave a playing deck of 32 cards.

● Trump suits rank with the Jack as the highest card, followed by the nine, Ace, ten, King, Queen, eight and seven (lowest). Non-trump suits rank with Ace as the highest card, followed by ten, King, Queen, Jack, nine, eight and seven (lowest).

● The seven of the trump suit is known as the 'Dix'.

▼ Suit ranking of trump suit (clubs)

High   Low
                                                                                        Dix

▼ Suit ranking of non-trump suit

High   Low

Dealing

The first dealer is chosen at random or by mutual consent. The dealer shuffles the cards and the non-dealer cuts them before the deal is made. Six cards are dealt, face-down, to each player in two packets of three. The next card is dealt face-up to the centre of the table (the 'upcard') and the remaining cards (the 'stock') are placed face-down next to it. Players are dealt three more cards after bidding (see Second deal below).

Bidding

● The upcard is the basis for the first round of bidding. Bidding starts with the non-dealer, who may call 'accept', 'pass' or 'schmeiss'. If the non-dealer accepts the upcard, the suit of that card becomes trumps. If the non-dealer passes, the dealer has a chance to accept the suit of the upcard as trumps or to pass. If the non-dealer calls 'schmeiss' he is proposing that a new deal be made. The dealer may then agree to a new deal, accept the suit of the upcard as trumps, or pass.

● If neither player accepts the suit of the upcard as trumps, and the players have not agreed to a new deal, the second round of bidding begins. The non-dealer may propose any suit, other than the suit of the upcard, as trumps, or pass. The dealer must accept the suit proposed by the non-dealer, or pass. If the non-dealer has passed, the dealer may propose a suit as trumps. If both players pass, the cards are reshuffled and a new deal is made.

● The player who decides the trump suit, either by accepting the upcard, proposing a suit or accepting a proposed suit, is known as the 'maker'.

Second deal

Once the trump suit has been decided, both players are dealt three more cards from the stock face-down one at a time. The bottom card of the stock is then placed face-up in the centre of the table. If either player holds the seven of the trump suit (the Dix) he may swap it for this card. This is not compulsory.

Sequences

● Players examine their cards to determine which sequences they have. A sequence is a run of three or more cards in the same suit. For the purposes of sequences, cards rank with the Ace highest, followed by the King, Queen, Jack, ten, nine, eight, seven (lowest).

● A sequence of three cards is worth 20 points. A sequence of four or more cards is worth 50 points. Sequences with the same points value are ranked according to the value of the highest card they contain. For example, the sequence Q♥, J♥, 10♥, is outranked by the sequence A♥, K♥, Q♥, because the highest card of the second sequence, A♥, is higher than the highest card of the first sequence Q♥. If two sequences are worth the same number of points and have the same highest card, the sequence made up of the trump suit wins. If neither of the equal sequences is in the trump suit, neither player receives points.

▶ Two sequences

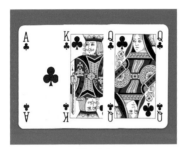

20 points

50 points

Declaring sequences

● Players declare their sequences before trick-taking play begins. The non-dealer begins the declaring process by declaring either 'sequence of twenty' if he has a three-card sequence, or 'sequence of fifty' if he has a card sequence of four or more.

● The dealer replies 'good' if he does not have a sequence worth more points, or 'not good' if he has a sequence that is worth more points, or 'how high?' if he has a sequence worth the same number of points. If the call is 'how high?', the non-dealer gives the name of the highest card in his sequence, to which the dealer replies 'good' if the highest card in his sequence is lower, or 'not good' if the highest-ranking card in his sequence is higher.

● The player with the highest-ranking sequence receives the points for that sequence once he has shown it to the other player. The other player receives no points at this stage. The winning declarer may also receive points for any other sequences he holds, but only if he is willing to show them to his opponent. This is not compulsory.

▶ A 19th-century French card depicting Hebe, goddess of youth

Playing

● The non-dealer begins the trick-taking phase by playing any card from his hand to the centre of the table. This is known as 'leading' the trick, while the suit of the first card played is known as the 'lead suit'.

● The dealer must contribute a card from the lead suit if he has one. If he has no card of the lead suit, he may play any other card including trump suit cards (assuming the lead suit and the trump suit are not the same).

● The trick is won by the highest-ranking card of the lead suit or the highest-ranking card of the trump suit if any were played. The winner of a trick, leads the next trick.

Bella

The King and Queen of the trump suit are known as the 'Bella'. Any player who holds the Bella wins 20 points, but only receives the points once both cards have been played to tricks. The Bella may also be included in sequences for normal point values.

◀ Bella

Scoring

Points can be won during play and after trick-taking play has ended.

Scoring during play

● Points may be won for sequences and for holding the Bella (see Declaring sequences, on the opposite page, and Bella, above).

● Points may also be won by capturing certain cards during trick-taking play. These cards and point values are shown in the table below:

CARD VALUES

Card	Points
Jack of trumps (the Jasz)	20
Nine of trumps (the Menel)	14
Ace (any suit)	11
10 (any suit)	10
King (any suit)	4
Queen (any suit)	3
Jack (except the Jasz)	2

10 points are also awarded to the player who wins the last trick.

Scoring the deal

● Once all nine tricks have been played, the total scores for the deal are calculated.

● If the maker has the higher score, both players keep the points they have won during play.

● If the maker's opponent has the higher score he is said to have 'gone bate' and scores the total of his own points and the maker's points (so the maker scores nothing).

● If the maker and his opponent have the same score, the maker's opponent is said to have 'gone half bate'; the maker scores nothing and his opponent scores half of his total points.

● The game is won by the first player to reach a cumulative total of 500 points or more scored from deals.

● If both players reach 500 points in the same deal, the player with the higher total wins. If both have equal scores, another deal is played as a decider.

Kalabriasz variants

▶ **FOUR-HANDED KALABRIASZ**
● Kalabriasz is often played as a four-player game.
● Players form two partnerships which remain constant throughout the game.

Dealing
● The dealership passes in a clockwise direction and must alternate between players from opposing partnerships.
● Players receive eight cards, except for the dealer who receives seven. Any player holding the Dix may exchange it for the upcard after the second deal. The dealer adds the Dix, or the original upcard if it has not been taken, to his hand before play begins.
● Bidding passes in a clockwise direction around the table (again alternating between players from opposing partnerships) and begins with the first player on the dealer's left.

Scoring
● The partner of the player who declares the highest sequence also scores points for any sequence that he holds.
● Partners keep a cumulative total of their combined scores for the purpose of scoring the deal.

Pinochle

Pinochle is a variant of Bezique and is a very popular trick-taking game in North America. The same game is sometimes known as Pinocle or Penuchle.

Objective

Players aim to win tricks that contain valuable cards and to complete melds with the cards they collect.

Card values

● Pinochle is played with a deck of 48 cards formed by combining the Aces, Kings, Queens, Jacks, tens and nines from two standard decks.

● The cards in a suit are ranked with the Ace highest, followed by ten, King, Queen, Jack and nine (lowest).

NUMBER OF CARDS

Two decks of 24 cards

RANKING ORDER

high

low

See text

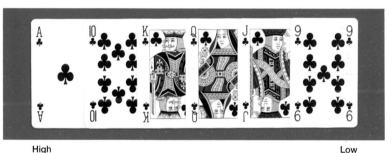

High   Low

◀ Card ranking

Dealing

● The first dealer is chosen at random, or by mutual consent, and the dealership subsequently alternates between the players. The cards are shuffled by the dealer and then cut by his opponent before the deal takes place.

● Both players receive twelve cards dealt face-down in three packets of four cards. The next card is dealt face-up to the centre of the table and is known as the 'upcard'. The suit of the upcard determines the trump suit for the deal. The remainder of the cards are placed face-down, so that the upcard is half-obscured, to form the stock.

Playing

● Play takes place in two stages, described in the following section: Stage one and Stage two.

Stage one

● Play begins with the dealer's opponent and alternates between the players. The first player places any card from his hand face-up on the table. This is known as 'leading' the trick. The suit of the lead card is known as the 'lead' suit of the trick. The next player may play any card from his hand to the trick.

● The trick is won by the highest-ranking card of the lead suit, if no trump cards are played, or by the highest-ranking trump card. If two identical cards are played, the player who led the trick wins. A player does not have to follow the lead suit and does not have to play a trump card if he chooses not to. The winner of a trick adds the top card of the stock to his hand and leads the next trick.

● When a player wins a trick, and after he has added the top card from the stock to his hand, he may use any of the cards in his hand to make a meld. To form a meld, a player must place the relevant cards face-up on the table and declare the name of the meld. There are three classes of meld, as shown below:

▶ Class A melds with diamonds as trumps

ⓐ Run or sequence
Ace, ten, King, Queen and Jack of the trump suit. Worth 150 points.
ⓑ Royal marriage
King and Queen of the trump suit. Worth 40 points.
ⓒ Marriage
King and Queen of any suit other than the trump suit. Worth 20 points.

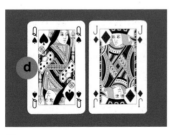

◀ Class B meld with diamonds as trumps

ⓓ Pinochle
Queen of spades and Jack of diamonds. Worth 40 points.

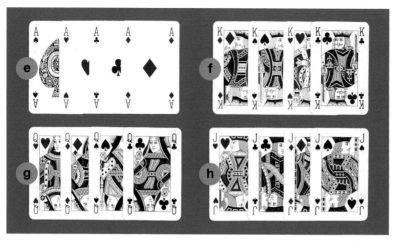

◀ Class C melds with diamonds as trumps

ⓔ Aces around
One Ace from each suit. Worth 100 points.
ⓕ Kings around
One King from each suit. Worth 80 points.
ⓖ Queens around
One Queen from each suit. Worth 60 points.
ⓗ Jacks around
One Jack from each suit. Worth 40 points.

● Only one meld may be made in each turn. Cards used in a meld may subsequently be used to play to a trick but cannot then be used to form part of a new meld. A card that has already been used in a meld may only be used to form a new meld of a different class, or a meld from the same class but with a higher points value in a later turn.

● There are special rules concerning the play of the nines of the trump suit, known as the 'Dix'. A Dix may be played instead of making a meld. To play the first Dix, a player exchanges it for the upcard (even if the upcard is the other Dix) and receives ten points. He may then make a meld in the regular manner. To play the second Dix, a player places it face-up on the table as if it were a meld and also receives ten points. He may not then make a regular meld in that turn. He may subsequently use the Dix to play to a trick in the same manner as any other melded card.

● Play continues in this manner until all the stock cards have been taken. The next player adds the upcard to his hand during his turn and may then choose to meld as normal.

● Melding is not compulsory. A player may choose not to show any potential melds he holds.

Stage two

- Stage two is sometimes referred to as the 'playoff' or the 'playout'. Both players gather all their cards into a single hand and use them to play twelve tricks. No melds are made at this stage of the game.
- The winner of the last trick of stage one leads the first trick of stage two. Subsequently, the winner of each trick leads the next.
- The trick-leader's opponent must play a card of the lead suit if he has one. If he does not have a card of the lead suit, he may play any other card, including trump cards. A trick is won by the highest-ranking card of the lead suit, if no trumps are played, or by the highest-ranking trump.

Scoring

- Points won by making melds are recorded as the melds are made. At the end of the second stage of play, points are awarded for tricks won that contain the following cards:

▶ Tricks containing these cards win points

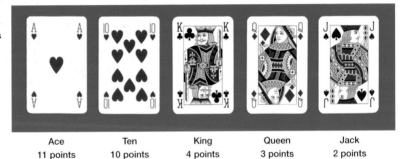

Ace	Ten	King	Queen	Jack
11 points	10 points	4 points	3 points	2 points

- The player who wins the last trick of the second stage gains an additional 10 points.
- The first player to accumulate 1000 points or more wins the game. In the event of a tie, points are awarded in the second stage according to the order in which tricks were taken, and the first player to reach 1000 points or more wins the game. Alternatively, a winner can be determined by continuing play to 1250 points. In the case of a second tie, play would continue to 1500 points, and so on, in increments of 250 points.
- Traditionally, points won for tricks are rounded up or down to the nearest ten points and the points value of Kings is raised to ten points. Effectively this means that Aces, tens and Kings all earn ten points, while Queens and Jacks earn nothing when scoring for tricks. This has the advantage of making all scores divisible by ten, so that the last zero can be ignored and all games played to 100 instead of 1000 points.

Pinochle variants

▶ AUCTION PINOCHLE

● Auction pinochle is an extended version of
Pinochle for four players that includes a
bidding phase.

Cards and dealing

● The same deck as that in Pinochle is used,
and the cards rank the same way within
their suits.

● The dealer takes no further part in a game
once the deal has been made. The
dealership passes in a clockwise direction.

● Each player receives fifteen cards in five
packets of three. Another packet of three
cards is then dealt face-down to the
centre of the table to form the 'widow'.

▲ A 19th-
century
English card

Bidding

● Beginning with the player to the
dealer's left, each player bids the number of
points he expects to win in that deal. Bidding usually begins at an
agreed minimum (300 points is reasonable) and proceeds in steps of ten
points.

● A player may pass rather than bid, but may then take no further
part in the bidding. Each bid must be higher than any previous bid.
Bidding ends when two players have passed. The last player to have
made a bid at that point is known as the 'bidder' and his last bid is
known as the 'contract'.

Melding

● The bidder turns the widow face-up and then adds the three cards
to his hand. He then declares the trump suit and lays down any melds
that he can achieve using any or all of the cards in his hand.

● Melds are scored in the same way as in Pinochle except that the Dix
counts as a class A meld worth ten points and is not exchanged for
another card.

● Only the bidder melds in games of Auction pinochle. The bidder may
rearrange and change his melds until he is satisfied that they represent
the maximum score. Melding is not compulsory.

Pinochle variants continued...

Playing
- There is only one stage of trick-taking play in Auction pinochle.
- The bidder begins play by placing three cards from his hand face-down on the table. He then collects all of his other cards and must play any one of them to lead the first trick. Play during a trick passes in a clockwise direction and the rules are the same as for the second stage of play in Pinochle. The winner of a trick leads the next trick.

Scoring
- Tricks are scored in the same way as they are in Pinochle, except that the winner of the last trick receives ten bonus points.
- The bidder receives any applicable points for the three cards he discarded face-down after melding.

The kitty
- Play in Auction pinochle is usually for chips or counters.
- Before play begins, players agree to contribute a set number of chips to the kitty at the start of each deal (three chips each is reasonable). If all three players pass during bidding, each puts an additional three chips into the kitty and a new deal is made.
- A bidder is paid by other players, or has to pay other players, depending on how successful he is at fulfilling the contract. A bidder is also paid from the kitty, or has to contribute to the kitty, again depending on how successful he is at fulfilling the contract.
- A bidder is always paid by the other players if he succeeds in winning at least as many points as his bid, and always pays the other players if he fails to win as many points as he has bid. A bidder is only paid from the kitty if he succeeds in fulfilling a contract of 350 points or more, and only pays into the kitty if he fails to fulfil a contract of 350 points or more. Payments are as listed in the table below:

Bid	Chips
300 – 340	3
350 – 390	5
400 – 440	10
450 – 490	15
500 – 540	20
550 – 590	25
600 or more	30

Piquet

Piquet is a classic trick-taking game for two players. It has been popular in Europe since at least the sixteenth century and the present-day French terminology used by English-speaking players is said to have been established under the reign of Charles I. The enduring popularity of Piquet is perhaps due to the great scope the game offers for players to develop their skills and strategies.

Objective

Players aim to win tricks and gain points by declaring specific combinations of cards in their hand.

Card values

● Piquet is played with a deck of 32 cards formed by removing all the sixes, fives, fours, threes and twos from a standard deck of 52 cards. A stripped deck of this kind is commonly referred to as a 'piquet deck' even when it is used in other card games.

● Cards in their suits rank with Ace highest, followed by King, Queen, Jack, ten, nine, eight and seven (lowest).

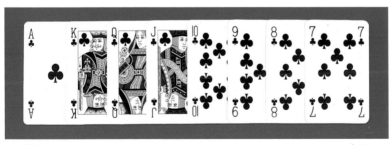

◀ Card ranking

High   Low

Dealing

● The first dealer is chosen at random, or by mutual consent, and the dealership subsequently alternates between the players. The dealer shuffles the cards and the non-dealer cuts them before the deal is made.

● Each player receives twelve cards, dealt face-down in six packets of two. The eight remaining cards are placed face-down on the table with the top five cards at an angle to the three on the bottom.

Playing

A game of Piquet is known as a 'partie' and consists of six deals. Each deal consists of three phases of play: discarding, declaring and trick-playing. Scoring takes place during the course of a partie, and at the end.

▲ A properly arranged stock

Discarding

● If a player has been dealt a hand that contains no court cards, he may declare the fact by calling 'carte blanche' and claim ten points. A carte blanche must be declared before either player discards.

● The dealer may discard up to five of his cards by placing them face-down on the table and adding the top five cards from the stock to his hand.

● If the dealer chooses to discard fewer then five cards, he has the right to look at the top five cards of the stock, but he takes only the same number of cards as he discarded. In this case, the dealer may not choose which of the top five cards to add to his hand; he must take them in the order they were dealt to the stock and also leave the remainder in their original order. A dealer must discard at least one card.

● The dealer's opponent must then discard at least one card. He may discard as many cards as there are remaining in the stock. The non-dealer's discards are placed face-down on the table and he replaces them with the same number of cards from the stock. If there are any cards left in the stock after both players have discarded, the non-dealer has the right to look at them. If the non-dealer decides to look at any cards remaining in the stock, he must show them to the dealer too.

Declaring

● There are three kinds of card combinations that players may form and declare from the cards in their hand. These are known as 'points', 'sequences' and 'melds'.

● A point is a group of non-consecutive cards from the same suit. The player with the largest number of cards in a point scores one for each card. If both players have points with the same number of cards, the total face value of all the cards in each point is calculated and the point with the highest value wins. For the purposes of counting total face values, cards have values as shown at the top of the facing page:

◀ Face values

Value = 11	Value = 10 each	Value = 9	Value = 8	Value = 7

EXAMPLE OF PLAY

Example of comparing points with the same number of cards:

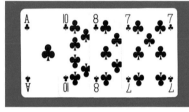 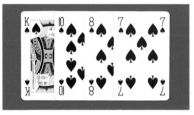

Point A   Point B

Point A

Point A contains 4 cards. The face values of the cards are 11 (Ace), 10 (ten), 8 (eight) and 7 (seven) making a total face value of 36.

Point B

Point B contains 4 cards. The face values of the cards are 10 (King), 10 (ten), 8 (eight) and 7 (seven) making a total face value of 35.

Point A has a higher total face value. The player who holds point A wins 4.

- If the total face values of two points are the same, neither player gains.
- A sequence is a collection of cards from the same suit that are consecutive according to rank order. The player with the longest sequence scores as follows:

POINT VALUES FOR SEQUENCES

Number of card	Score	Number of card	Score
3 (tierce)	3	7 (septième)	17
4 (quart)	4	8 (huitième)	18
5 (quint)	15		
6 (sixième)	16		

89

● If both players have sequences of the same length, the sequence that contains the highest-ranking card wins.

EXAMPLES OF PLAY

Example 1 of comparing sequences with the same number of cards:

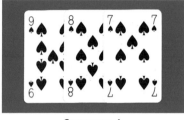 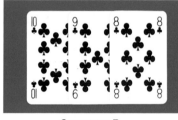

Sequence A   Sequence B

Both sequences contain 3 cards, but sequence B has the highest-ranking card (a ten), so the player holding sequence B earns 3 points.

Example 2 of comparing sequences with the same number of cards:

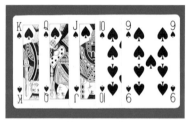 

Sequence C   Sequence D

Both sequences contain 5 cards, but sequence D has the highest-ranking card (an Ace), so the player holding sequence D earns 15 points.

● If both players hold sequences of the same length with the same top-ranking card, neither player gains points.

● A meld is a collection of three or four cards of the same rank from different suits. Only Aces, Kings, Queens, Jacks and tens may be used to form melds. Some players only allow tens to be used to form melds of four cards.

● If both players hold melds containing the same number of cards, the meld with the highest-ranking card wins. If both players hold melds with the same number of cards of the same rank, neither player gains points.

● Melds are awarded points as shown in the table at the top of the opposite page:

POINT VALUES FOR MELDS

Number of card	Score
3 (trio)	3
4 (quatorze)	14

Trio

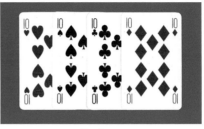

Quatorze

● The calls that should be used to declare collections of cards are designed to prevent either player gaining any more than the minimum possible information about their opponent's hand.

Declaring points

● The non-dealer begins by declaring his highest-value point by calling 'a point of (number of cards)'. If the dealer does not hold a point with more cards, he calls 'good', conceding that he cannot beat the point. If he holds a point containing more cards, he calls 'not good, a point of (number of cards)'. If he holds a point with the same number of cards he calls 'how many?'. If the dealer calls 'how many?' his opponent calls 'a point of (number of cards), I score (total face value of cards)'. The dealer must reply 'good' if the total face value of his point is less, 'not good, a point of (number of cards), I score (total face value of cards)' if the total face value of his point is greater, or 'equal' if the total face value is the same.

● A player who wins a point declaration always closes by restating 'a count of (number of cards), I score (total face value of cards)'.

Declaring sequences

● The non-dealer continues by declaring his highest-value sequence. This is done by calling 'a sequence of (number of cards)'. The dealer may reply with 'good', 'not good, a sequence of (number of cards)' or 'how high?'. If the call is 'how high?' the non-dealer must reply with the name of his top-ranking card. Otherwise, dialogue is the same as for declaring points.

Declaring melds

● The non-dealer continues by declaring his highest-value meld. This is done by calling 'a (three or fourteen) of (card rank)'. The dealer may reply with 'good' or 'not good'. It is not possible for two players to have the same melds. Otherwise, dialogue is the same as for declaring points.

EXAMPLE OF PLAY

Example of a properly-conducted declaration:

Non-dealer: 'A point of four' (he holds a point containing four cards).
Dealer: 'Good' (he does not hold a point containing four or more cards).
Non-dealer: 'A point of four, I score four' (he scores one for each card in the point). 'A sequence of five' (he holds a sequence containing five cards).
Dealer: 'How high?' (he also holds a sequence containing five cards).
Non-dealer: 'Jack' (the highest-ranking card in his sequence is a Jack).
Dealer: 'Not good' (the highest-ranking card in his sequence is higher than a Jack).
Non-dealer: 'A trio of Queens' (he holds a meld of three Queens).
Dealer: 'Not good' (he holds a higher-ranking meld).

The non-dealer then plays the first card to the first trick. He scores four for his combinations (he only scores for his point of four) plus one for leading the first trick (see Trick playing on the opposite page).

Non-dealer: 'I start with five' (he has a total of five points).

The dealer then makes his declarations.

Dealer: 'A quart to Queen (a sequence of four cards with a Queen as the highest-ranking card), also a tierce (a second sequence of three cards with the highest card undeclared). Eight (he scores eight points for the two sequences). A quatorze of kings (a meld of four kings). Fourteen (he scores an additional fourteen points for the meld). I start with twenty-two (he has a total of twenty-two points).

● Only the player with the highest-ranking combination for each of the three classes of combinations (points, sequences and melds) scores for that class of combinations. If a player holds the highest-ranking combination in a class, he also scores for any other combinations in the same class that he holds.

- A player is allowed to conceal the fact that he holds a particular combination by not declaring it. This is known as 'sinking'. A player may only sink one of his combinations.

Trick playing

- The non-dealer begins trick play as soon as he has finished declaring. To begin, he places any card from his hand face-up on the table. This is known as 'leading' the trick, and the suit of that card is known as the 'lead' suit for the trick. The non-dealer receives one point for leading the first trick.
- The next player must play a card of the same suit as the lead suit if he has one. Otherwise he may play any other card.
- A trick is won by the highest-ranking card of the lead suit. Points are scored during trick-play as shown in the table below:

POINTS FOR TRICK PLAY

Play	Score
Leading a trick	1
Winning a trick led by the opponent	1
Winning the last trick	1
Winning seven or more tricks	10
Winning all twelve tricks (capot)	40

A player who wins a capot, does not also receive ten points for winning seven tricks

Scoring

- Points scored during the declaration and during trick play are announced and recorded as they are gained. Two additional point bonuses are available during play, known as 'pique' and 'repique' bonuses. If the non-dealer scores 30 points before the dealer has scored, he receives a pique bonus of 30 points. If a player scores 30 points before the first trick is led, he receives a repique bonus of 60 points. These bonuses are also announced and recorded during play. A player may claim both bonuses if he is eligible.
- Cumulative scores for each deal are recorded, then all six totals are added together at the end of the partie. A player with a combined total of less than 100 points is said to have been 'rubiconed'. If both players have 100 or more points, the game is won by the player with the higher

score. The winner's final score is the difference between his total points and his opponent's total points plus a bonus of 100 points for winning the partie. If one or both players are rubiconed, the player with the higher score wins the game. The winner's final score is the sum of his total points and his opponent's total points plus a bonus of 100 points for winning the partie.

EXAMPLES OF PLAY

Examples of partie scoring:

	Total points	Final score	
Dealer	120	120 - 108 + 100 = 112	winner
Non-dealer	108	0	
Dealer	95	0	
Non-dealer	125	125 + 95 + 100 = 320	winner
Dealer	85	85 + 82 + 100 = 267	winner
Non-dealer	82	0	

MUST KNOW

Strategy tips

● The discard phase is critical. The dealer is in a much stronger position than the non-dealer at this point and should normally take the maximum five cards to try to build the strongest hand possible. The non-dealer generally has to play defensively, so the dealer should not normally bother thinking about defence. Taking all five cards increases the dealer's chance of forming a winning point and a winning sequence and therefore increases his chances of making a pique or repique bonus.

● It is a good idea for a player to retain cards from the suit that makes up the majority in their hand. In a hand with no dominant suit, the suit that is more likely to form a winning point or sequence should be retained. Aces and cards that are likely to form winning melds (trios or quatorzes) should also generally be retained.

● Be aware of which melds your opponent cannot possibly have, based on the contents of your own hand. For example, if you hold a meld of four Jacks as well as at least one Ace, King and Queen in various suits, you know that meld cannot be beaten since your opponent cannot hold a superior four-card meld of Aces, Kings, or Queens.

● Always take an opportunity to win a repique.

Piquet variants

► **PIQUET AU CENT**
- Piquet au cent is a variant of Piquet with a different system of scoring the partie.

Scoring
- There is no fixed number of deals in a partie. Play continues until one player reaches 100 points. The hand is finished, and any additional points are awarded before the game is finally scored.
- The player with the highest score at the end of the last deal wins and scores the difference between his own and his opponent's totals.
- If the winner's opponent's total is less than 50, the winner's final score is doubled.

► **AUCTION PIQUET**
- Auction piquet is a variant of Piquet that includes a bidding phase and has a slightly different scoring method.

Bidding
- Before the discard takes place, the non-dealer must make a bid or pass. The dealer may then make a bid or pass. If both players pass, the cards are reshuffled and redealt by the next player.
- A player's bid specifies the number of tricks he expects to win or lose. The minimum bid is seven and bids must be for more tricks than any previous bid.
- A bid may be a 'minus' bid or a 'plus' bid. A minus bid is a prediction that the player making the bid will lose the number of tricks he mentions. A plus bid is a prediction that the player making the bid will win the number of tricks he mentions.
- The winning bid is the bid that states the highest number of tricks regardless of whether it is a minus bid or a plus bid.
- Bidding ends as soon as one player passes and the last bid made becomes the contract, which the player who made it must try to fulfil.

Doubling and redoubling
- A player may call 'double' after any bid made by his opponent, meaning that he believes he can prevent the other player from fulfilling that bid if it became the contract. A bidder may reply to a call of 'double' by calling 'redouble' if he believes that his opponent would not be able to stop him fulfilling such a contract.

95

Piquet variants continued...

- Doubles and redoubles are cancelled by any subsequent bid to win or lose a higher number of tricks than the number of tricks cited in the doubled or redoubled bid.

Playing

- Players are not required to discard any cards.
- Declarations are made in any order rather than points, followed by sequences, followed by melds.
- A player may not sink (conceal) a declaration if he has won a bid for a minus contract.
- The pique bonus is scored by any player who gains 21 points before his opponent scores during play for a minus contract and by any player who gains 29 points under the same conditions during a plus contract.
- The repique bonus is scored by any player who gains 21 points before the first trick is led when playing for a minus contract, and by any player who gains 30 points under the same conditions during a plus contract.

Scoring

- A player earns one point for every trick he wins.
- No points are awarded for leading a trick, and there are no

▼ Cards from an early 19th-century deck depicting
great Kings from history, their Queens and sons

no additional points awarded to a player who wins the last trick.

● A winning bidder scores ten points for every trick in excess of the contract that he wins for a plus contract, or ten points for every trick in excess of the contract that he loses for a minus contract. These extra tricks are known as 'overtricks'.

● The winning bidder's opponent scores ten points for every trick less than the number of tricks the bidder contracted to win for plus contracts, or ten points for every trick less than the number of tricks the bidder contracted to lose for a minus contract. These missing tricks are known as 'undertricks'.

● If a player fulfils a contract that was doubled by his opponent, he doubles the score for overtricks (20 points each). If a player fails to fulfil a contract that was doubled by his opponent, his opponent receives double points for undertricks (20 points each).

● If a player fulfils a contract that he redoubled, he redoubles the score for overtricks (40 points each). If a player fails to fulfil a contract that he redoubled, his opponent receives redoubled points for undertricks (40 points each).

● Scoring the partie is the same as for Piquet, except that a player is said to be rubiconed if his total is less than 150 points, and a player who wins the partie receives a bonus of 150 points.

games

for three

Adding a third player can make for a challenging gaming session. The tactics and strategy needed for a three-player game are far subtler than for a two-player game. Treachery and last-minute twists of fate are to be expected.

All fours

NUMBER OF CARDS

52

One deck of 52 cards

All fours originated in England during the seventeenth century. The game later spread to the United States, became very popular there in the nineteenth century, and eventually gave rise to many variants. A version of All fours is the national card game of Trinidad and the same or similar games with names such as Seven up, High-low Jack and Old sled remain popular across the English-speaking world today.

RANKING ORDER

high

low

Objective

To gain points by winning tricks that contain certain cards.

Card values

A standard deck of 52 cards is used. The cards in a suit rank with the Ace highest, followed by King, Queen, Jack, ten, nine, eight, seven, six, five, four, three and two (lowest).

▶ Card ranking for any suit

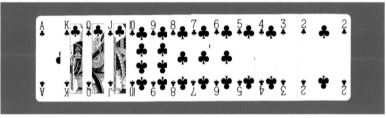

High   Low

Dealing

● The first dealer is chosen at random, or by mutual consent, and the dealership subsequently passes in a clockwise direction. The cards are shuffled by the player to the dealer's right and cut by the player to the dealer's left before the deal is made.

● Six cards are dealt, face-down, to each player in two packets of three. The next card is dealt face-up to the centre of the table and is known as the 'upcard'. If the upcard is a Jack of any suit, the dealer gains one point.

Deciding trumps

● The upcard is the basis for deciding trumps. The player to the dealer's left has the opportunity to call 'stand', if he wants the suit of the upcard to become trumps, at which point trick-taking play begins, or 'I beg' if he does not want it to become trumps. After a call of 'I beg' the dealer has the choice of retaining the suit of the upcard as trumps by calling 'take one', which entitles the player to his left to one point and starts trick-taking play with that suit as trumps, or to continue the deal.

● If the dealer decides to continue the deal, a packet of three more cards is dealt to each player and the next card is dealt face-up to the centre of the table as a new upcard. If the suit of the new upcard is different from the suit of the old upcard, that suit becomes trumps and trick-taking play begins. If the suit of the new upcard is the same as the old upcard, the dealer repeats the process of dealing packets of three cards to each player followed by a new upcard until a new suit is revealed. If the upcard that finally decides the trump suit is a Jack, the dealer gains one point. If no new suit is revealed before the dealer runs out of cards, the deck is reshuffled and passed to the next dealer.

Playing

● If an extended deal takes place in order to decide the trump suit, all players must discard enough cards for each to be left with a hand of six cards only (any cards may be discarded).

● The player to the dealer's left begins and play subsequently passes in a clockwise direction. The first player is said to 'lead' the trick. He places any card from his hand face-up on the table. The suit of that card is known as the 'lead' suit for the trick.

● The next player must contribute a card belonging to the lead suit if he has one. If he has no cards of the lead suit, he may play any other card including trump cards. The trick ends when all three players have contributed one card.

● The trick is won by the player who contributed the highest-ranked card of the lead suit, if no trump cards were played, or the highest-ranked trump card. The winner of a trick leads the next trick. The deal ends once all six tricks have been played.

Scoring

All tricks are turned face-up at the end of a deal to determine scoring. One point is awarded for any player holding:

    a) High – the highest trump
    b) Low – the lowest trump
    c) Jack – the Jack of the trump suit
    d) Game – the cards with the highest cumulative value

For the purposes of scoring Game, certain cards have point values as shown in the table below:

CARD VALUES

Card	Value
Ace (any suit)	4
King (any suit)	3
Queen (any suit)	2
Jack (any suit)	1
Ten (any suit)	10

Winning

The first player to reach seven points wins the game. As one player nears a total of seven points, scoring is carried out in the strict order of 'High', 'Low', 'Jack' and 'Game'. In other words points are awarded for these holdings in the same order as the tricks that contain them are won. If a player captures the Jack of the trump suit in the first trick, he receives a point before a player who captures, for example, the highest trump in a subsequent trick.

MUST KNOW

Strategy tips

• The dealer is in a powerful position because he has more influence over the choice of the upcard than the other players. The trump suit determines two of the four points that are available in a deal: 'High' and 'Low'.

• A player's decision about whether to accept or reject the first upcard must clearly be based on his hand. The ideal hand would contain an Ace and a two of the same suit as the upcard because that would guarantee a point for both High and Low. Failing that, a hand containing an Ace of the same suit as the upcard and two or three other cards of the same suit in sequence or near sequence is the most desirable.

• Players should always bear in mind that capturing tricks that contain point-scoring cards (the highest trump, the lowest trump and the Jack of the trump suit) is more important than the sheer number of tricks won. Winning more tricks than your opponents may secure you a point for 'Game', but capturing a trick that contains the Jack of the trump suit will always win you a point.

• If you hold the Ace or Jack of the trump suit, it is better to save that card until the last trick if you can. It is more likely to win the last trick than the first and will then remain in your possession.

Five hundred

Five hundred was invented in the United States at the beginning of the twentieth century. Today, it is regarded as the national card game of Australia, where it is also played as a four-person game. Five hundred is based on the four-player game Euchre (see page 148).

Objective

Players compete in a bidding phase and then try to fulfil their bid in trick-taking play if successful.

Card values

● All cards with a face-value below seven are removed from a standard deck and one Joker is added to create a playing deck of 33 cards.

● When trumps are in play, the Joker is the highest-ranking card of the trump suit, followed by the Jack of the trump suit and then the Jack of the suit of the same colour as the trump suit (black or red). Following these, the other cards rank from Ace (highest) down to seven (lowest). The Jack of the trump suit is known as 'Right bower', and the Jack of the same colour as the trump suit as 'Left bower'.

ⓐ Right bower   **ⓑ** Left bower

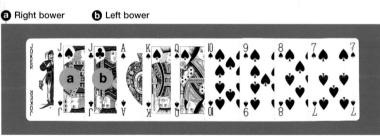

High   Low

◀ Card ranking with spades as trumps

● The cards of the other suits rank with Ace highest followed by King, Queen, Jack (unless part of the trump suit because it is the same colour), ten, nine, eight and seven (lowest).

● When trumps are not in play the cards in all suits rank with Ace highest followed by King, Queen, Jack, ten, nine, eight and seven. The Joker is nominated to a particular suit and becomes the highest-ranking card in that suit (see Playing the Joker, page 106). The suits are ranked with no trumps highest, followed by hearts, diamonds, clubs and spades (lowest).

► Card
ranking of
all suits with
no trumps
and Joker
nominated
to clubs

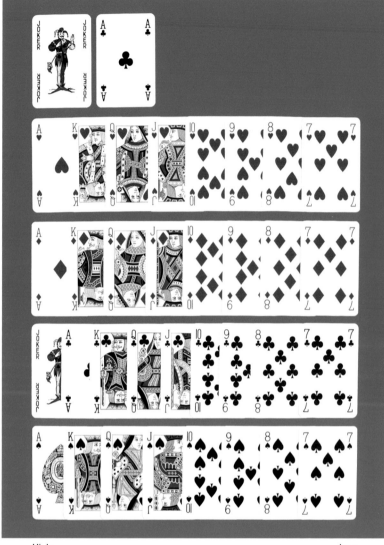

High   Low

Dealing

● The first dealer is chosen at random and the dealership subsequently
passes in a clockwise direction. The cards are shuffled by the player to the
dealer's right and cut by the player to his left before the deal begins.

● Ten cards are dealt to each player and three are dealt to the 'widow' in
the centre of the table. A packet of three cards is dealt to each player,
followed by one to the widow, then three more to each player and another

to the widow, and finally four to each player and the last card to the widow. All cards are dealt face-down.

Bidding

● Bidding begins with the player to the dealer's left and passes in a clockwise direction. A player may bid the number of tricks he believes he can win and nominate a trump suit, or the number of tricks he believes he can win and nominate to play with no trump suit (no trumps). Bids may be for a minimum of six tricks or a maximum of ten.

● A player may pass rather than bid, but passing once precludes that player from making any further bids. If all three players pass, the cards are reshuffled and passed to the next dealer. The bidding phase ends when two players have passed. The remaining player's bid becomes the bid for the game and that player is known as the 'declarer'.

● A bid must be higher than any previous bid. This means that it must be a bid to take more tricks or a bid to take the same number of tricks in a higher-ranking suit. The lowest possible bid is six spades (six tricks with spades, the lowest-ranking trump) and the highest is ten no trump (ten tricks with no trumps, the highest-ranking trump).

EXAMPLE OF PLAY

Example of possible bidding:

Player A	Player B	Player C
6♠	6♣	7♠
8♠	PASS	9♠
PASS		

1 Player A opens the bidding with 6♠ (the lowest possible bid).
2 Player B makes a higher bid of 6♣ (clubs outranks spades).
3 Player C raises the bid again to 7♠ (the number of tricks bid is higher).
4 Player A tops player C's bid with 8♠.
5 Player B passes (he cannot bid again) and player C raises his bid to 9♠.
6 Player A passes. Two players have passed, so the bidding ends. Player C is the declarer with a bid of 9♠ (an undertaking to win 9 tricks with spades as trumps).

Playing

● Play begins with the declarer and proceeds in a clockwise direction. The declarer picks up the three cards of the widow, adds them to his hand and then discards any three cards face-down (including any widow cards).

- The declarer plays any card from his hand to start the first trick. The suit of that card is the 'lead' suit of the trick. Subsequent players must contribute a card of the same suit if they have one. If they have no cards of the lead suit, they may play any card, including a trump card.
- The trick is won by the player who contributed the highest-ranked card of the lead suit if no trump cards were played, or the highest-ranked trump card.

Playing the Joker

- If the winning bid was for no trumps and the declarer holds the Joker, he may nominate a suit for it. The Joker then becomes the highest-ranking card in that suit. If the winning bid was no trumps and one of the declarer's opponents holds the Joker, or if the declarer chooses not to nominate a suit, the Joker becomes the highest-ranking card in the deck and wins any trick to which it is played. The Joker may only be played to a trick if the player who holds it has no cards of the lead suit in that trick.
- If the winning bid named a suit as trumps, the Joker becomes the highest-ranking card in the trump suit regardless of who holds it.

Scoring

- A declarer wins the deal if he wins at least as many tricks as he bid. A declarer who wins a deal receives points depending on his bid:

POINT VALUES

Tricks bid	Spades	Clubs	Diamonds	Hearts	No trumps
Six	40	60	80	100	120
Seven	140	160	180	200	220
Eight	240	260	280	300	320
Nine	340	360	380	400	420
Ten	440	460	480	500	520

- The declarer's opponents gain ten points for every trick they win whether the declarer fulfils his bid or not.
- A declarer who fails to win as many tricks as he bid, loses rather than gains the number of points indicated for his bid in the table above.
- If the declarer wins every trick, this is known as a 'slam', and he gains 250 points if the value of his bid was less than 250 points. If the value of his bid was 250 points or more, there is no extra bonus for making a slam.

- The first player whose cumulative point total reaches 500 points or more wins the game. If more than one player has a total of 500 or more points at the end of a deal, the player who first reached 500 points during the course of the deal wins.

MUST KNOW

Strategy tips

- Most deals are won by hands that include five or more trumps, a fact that should be borne in mind when bidding.
- A simple but approximate method of calculating how many tricks a hand is likely to win is to add the number of trump cards it contains to the number of non-trump Aces and Kings. On average, a hand will win the same number of tricks as this total.
- It is best to bid no trumps only if you hold a hand that has a long sequence, or near sequence, of one suit.
- The chances of finding a specific card in the widow are low (about one in six or seven), so it is unwise to make a bid that relies on collecting a specific card from the widow to be fulfilled. However the chances of finding at least one card in the widow that will strengthen a hand (enable one extra trick to be won) are good.
- After taking the widow it is a good idea to discard cards from suits with shorter runs rather than cards from suits with longer runs. Cards that do not form part of any run are usually the ideal discards.

Five hundred variants

▶ **FOUR-HANDED FIVE HUNDRED**

- In Australia, Five hundred is commonly played with four players.
- A deck of 43 cards is used, formed by adding the sixes, the fives and two of the fours (one red, one black) to the deck used in the three-handed game.
- The four players form two partnerships that are fixed for the duration of the game. Partners sit opposite each other during play.
- Bids are made on the basis of the performance of the partnership rather than the individual player. A player bidding, for example, six spades is committing his partnership to winning six tricks with spades as trumps.
- Bidding and play is the same as in the three-handed game, except that players cooperate with their partners. The game ends when one partnership reaches a cumulative total of 500 points or more.

Pope Joan

Pope Joan is a traditional British card game that was very
popular in the eighteenth and nineteenth centuries – Charles
Dickens has his characters playing Pope Joan in a chapter
of The Pickwick Papers. The earliest references to the game
are from around 1730 and it probably evolved from earlier
games called Hoc and Comet. It is not clear how the game
came to be named after a legendary female pope from the
ninth century. The nine of diamonds, a key card in the game,
is also traditionally known as 'the curse of Scotland' for
equally mysterious reasons.

Objective

To gain counters by playing certain cards to become the first player to
discard all his cards.

Card values

- The eight of diamonds is removed from a standard deck leaving a
playing deck of 51 cards. The nine of diamonds is known as 'Pope Joan'.
- Aces are the lowest-ranking cards and Kings are the highest.

► Card
ranking for
any suit

Pope Joan

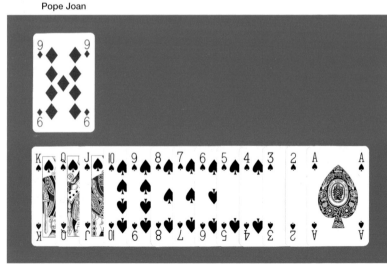

High   Low

Preparing

All players will need an equal number of counters (at least twenty each) and a board for betting. Purpose-made boards are available commercially and there many examples of antique Pope Joan boards, but an adequate board can easily be drawn up on a large piece of paper or card as shown in the example below.

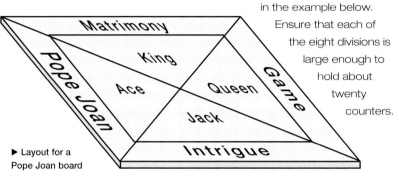

▶ Layout for a
Pope Joan board

Ensure that each of the eight divisions is large enough to hold about twenty counters.

Betting

Before the deal takes place, each player places an equal number of counters on each of the eight divisions of the board. Players must agree on the actual number of counters before the game begins (one or two would be a reasonable number).

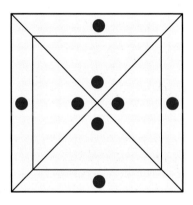

◀ One player's bet on the board (one counter per division)

Dealing

● The first dealer is chosen at random, or by mutual consent, and the dealership subsequently passes in a clockwise direction. The cards are shuffled by the player to the dealer's right and cut by the player to the dealer's left before the deal is made.

● The cards are dealt face-down and one at a time. Cards are dealt to a fourth hand before they are dealt to the dealer's own hand. This fourth hand remains face-down and untouched throughout play. The last card is dealt face-up to the centre of the table and is known as the 'upcard'. Players will not have the same number of cards.

● If the upcard is the nine of diamonds (Pope Joan), the dealer automatically collects all the counters in the Pope Joan and Game division of the board and the cards are reshuffled and redealt by the next dealer.

● If the upcard is any card other than Pope Joan, the suit of that card becomes the trump suit of the deal. If the upcard is an Ace, King, Queen, or Jack, all the counters on the corresponding division of the board go to the dealer, but play continues with the suit of that card as the lead suit.

Playing

● Play begins with the player to the dealer's left. The first player may play any card from his hand by placing it face-up on the centre of the table. Whoever has the next card of the same suit in sequence must then play that card. Play continues in this way until no player has a card that can continue the sequence. If a player has more than one consecutive card in the sequence, he must play all of them at the same time. A sequence will end, or reach a 'stop' when:

a) The last card played is a King, because there are no more cards in the ranking sequence after the King.

b) The next card in the sequence will be the eight of diamonds, because it is not part of the Pope Joan playing deck.

c) No player has the next card in the sequence because it has already been played or because it is in the fourth, concealed, hand.

● When the end of a sequence is reached, the cards of that sequence are turned face-down and the player who contributed the last card to the sequence begins another sequence with any card from his hand.

● Sequences of one card are possible.

Claiming counters

● Certain cards win counters from the board when they are played. Any player who plays the Ace, King, Queen or Jack of the trump suit individually wins all the counters from that division on the board. Playing the Jack and Queen of the trump suit at the same time wins all the counters from the Jack division, the Queen division, and the Intrigue division of the board. Playing the King and Queen of the trump suit at the same time wins all the counters from the King division, the Queen division, and the Matrimony division of the board. Playing the Pope Joan wins all the counters from the Pope Joan division of the board.

● Counters are claimed for all the cards played at the same time so that, in the unlikely event that a player added the Jack, Queen, and King to a sequence, he would receive counters from each of the corresponding divisions plus the Matrimony and Intrigue divisions.

● These cards only win counters when they are played; counters cannot be claimed while cards are still in the hand.

▼ Counters may be claimed from these divisions when the cards below are played (spades are trumps)

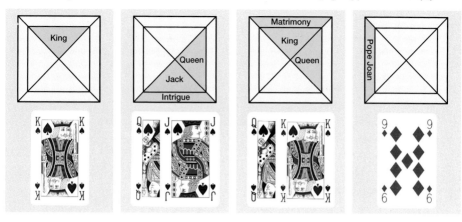

Ending the round

The round ends when one player plays his last card. This is known as 'going out'. A player who goes out collects all the counters from the Game division of the board plus any other counters that card may entitle him to. All other players must pay one counter for every card they still hold to a player who goes out, unless they hold Pope Joan, in which case they pay nothing. Unclaimed counters on the board remain where they are for the next round and new counters are added by each player in the same way that they were before the start of the first round (see Preparing, page 109).

Ending the game

● Play continues for a set number of rounds agreed before the game begins. A final round is then played. No counters are added to the board before the final round. If there are no counters left on the board, no final round is played.

● In the final round, there is no concealed fourth hand and the final card is dealt to a player, so there is no trump suit. Players who are dealt the Ace, King, Queen and Jack of diamonds and Pope Joan claim the counters from the relevant divisions of the board. Counters in the Matrimony division go to a player who holds both the King and the Queen of diamonds, or are shared equally between the two players who hold them. Counters in the Intrigue division go to a player who holds both the Queen and Jack of diamonds, or are shared equally between the two players who hold them.

● If there is an uneven number of counters in a division that is to be shared, the odd counter goes to the player who holds the higher-ranking of the two cards.

Pope Joan variants

▶ **BETTING**

● In some games, players are required to place more than one counter on some of the divisions of the board before play begins. A common variant requires players to place four on Pope Joan, two on Intrigue and Matrimony, and one on each of the other divisions.

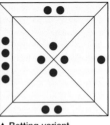
▲ Betting variant

▶ **NEW SEQUENCES**

● One variant requires a player to start a new sequence in a different suit from the previous sequence.

● Another variant requires that all sequences, including the first of the game, must start with the lowest card of a particular suit held by the player who is starting a sequence.

▶ **CLAIMING COUNTERS**

● In some games, the counters in the Matrimony and Intrigue divisions are shared between players who play the Jack and Queen or the Queen and King of the trump suit after one another. In the case where there is an uneven number of counters, the odd counter goes to the player of the higher-ranking card.

▶ **POPE JOAN HOLDER**

● In some games, a player who is holding Pope Joan when another player goes out is not excused from paying that player. Instead the player holding Pope Joan must pay two counters for every card he still has in his hand.

▶ **POPE JOAN BOARD**

● Some players use the cards from a second deck instead of a Pope Joan board with divisions. The Ace, King, Queen, Jack and nine of diamonds are placed face-up to represent the Ace, King, Queen, Jack and Pope Joan divisions of the board. The Intrigue division is represented by the Jack and Queen of one of the black suits, and the Matrimony division by the King and Queen of the other black suit. The Game division is represented by a Joker.

● Counters are stacked on or by the relevant cards for the purposes of betting.

Preference

Preference is a traditional, trick-taking game played throughout Central Europe and Russia. There is a Croatian and several Russian versions of the game. Preference differs from other trick-taking games in that play is traditionally for a 'pot', which can either be money or, more commonly, chips or markers.

Objective

Players compete to make the highest bid and then play to fulfil their bid or to prevent an opponent from fulfilling a bid.

Card values

● All cards with a face value below seven are removed from a standard deck to create a playing deck of 32 cards.

● All suits are ranked with Ace highest, followed by King, Queen, Jack, ten, nine, eight and seven (lowest).

● The suits are ranked with hearts (known as 'Preference') as the highest, followed by diamonds, then clubs then spades (lowest).

◄ Card ranking for any suit

High   Low

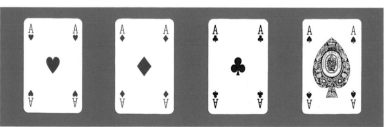

◄ Suit ranking

High   Low
Preference

PREFERENCE

113

Preparation

Play is for chips or coins contributed by each player to form a pot. Before a game begins, players must decide how many chips must be contributed by each player before play begins (ten is reasonable), how many chips should be paid out of the pot to a player who fulfils his bid (five multiplied by the value of the bid is reasonable) and how many chips a player who fails to fulfil his bid must pay in (again, five multiplied by the value of the bid is reasonable).

Dealing

● The first dealer is selected at random, or by mutual consent, and the dealership subsequently passes in a clockwise direction. The player to the dealer's right shuffles the cards and the player to the dealer's left cuts them before the deal is made.

● Each player receives ten face-down cards, and two are dealt face-down to the table to form the 'Talon'. A packet of three cards is first dealt to each player, followed by one to the Talon, followed by a packet of four cards to each player, another to the Talon and then a final packet of three to each player.

Bidding

● The player to the dealer's left begins bidding, which then continues in a clockwise direction. The first player may pass or bid one of the four suits. Subsequent players may also pass or bid a suit, but they may only bid a suit that is higher in rank than any previously bid suit. If two players pass, the suit bid by the other player becomes the trump suit and that player has undertaken to win at least six tricks with that trump suit.

● If all three players pass, a second round of bidding begins. A player may pass or put chips into the pot. The player who puts the largest number of chips into the pot wins the right to name the trump suit and undertakes to win at least six tricks with that trump suit. That player may also add the Talon to his hand and discard any two cards (including Talon cards). The Talon is only available to the winning bidder if the bidding goes to a second round. The player who names trumps is known as the 'declarer'.

● For the purposes of bidding, the suits are valued in their rank order, so that spades are worth one, clubs two, diamonds three and hearts four. These numbers are multipliers for the purpose of paying out of, or into, the pot at the end of trick-taking play. For example, a declarer who has made a bid of diamonds stands to win or lose three multiplied by five (assuming five has been agreed) chips.

Playing

- The player to the declarer's left begins and play subsequently passes in a clockwise direction. The first player is said to 'lead' the trick. He places any card from his hand face-up on the table. The suit of that card is known as the 'lead' suit for the trick.
- The next player must contribute a card belonging to the lead suit if he has one. If he has no cards of the lead suit, he may play any other card including trump cards.
- The trick is won by the player who contributed the highest-ranked card of the lead suit, if no trump cards were played, or the highest-ranked trump card. The winner of a trick leads the next trick. The deal ends once all ten tricks have been played.

EXAMPLE OF PLAY

Example of possible trick-taking play with diamonds as trumps:

1 Player A, to the left of the declarer, leads the trick with 7♠. Spades are the lead suit of the trick.
2 Player B follows the lead suit by playing 9♠.
3 Player C, the declarer, has no spades and is therefore allowed to play any other card. He plays 6♦.
4 Player C wins the trick because he played the only, and therefore the highest-ranking, trump card. If player C had not had a trump card, player B would have won the trick because his card was the highest-ranking in the lead suit.

Settling

Play is for chips from the pot, so there are no points as such. A declarer who fulfils his bid is paid from the pot according to the table below. A declarer who fails to fulfil his bid pays the same number of chips into the pot as he would have won if he had fulfilled his bid.

NULL GAME VALUES

Trump suit	Trump suit value	x	Agreed units	=	Units to pay/receive
Hearts	4		5		20
Diamonds	3		5		15
Clubs	2		5		10
Spades	1		5		5

5 units are assumed as the agreed price or prize.

Preference variants

▶ **BIDDING VARIANTS**
- More complex forms of bidding are used in some Preference variants.
- The lowest possible bid must be made first and subsequent bids must be in the order of the bid ranking: players are not allowed to skip to a higher-ranking bid.
- The first player to bid has the choice of the following calls:

Pass
The player declines to make a bid and may not make any further bids.
Spades
A bid to win six tricks with spades as trumps and to pick up the Talon. Spades is the lowest possible bid, since it is only worth one. The first player cannot bid the higher-ranking clubs or diamonds.
Game
A bid to nominate the trump suit (other than hearts) and win six tricks without looking at the Talon.
Hearts
A bid to win six tricks with hearts as trumps without looking at the Talon.

- A bid of hearts by any player immediately ends bidding. The second player may bid clubs (the next-lowest bid after spades), game or hearts, or he may pass. The next player may bid diamonds (the next-lowest bid after clubs) game or hearts, or he may pass. A player may not bid game or hearts if he has previously bid a suit. If a player bids game, the only possible bid that can beat it is hearts.
- After a successful suit bid, the declarer adds the Talon to his hand and discards any two cards (including Talon cards). He may at this point nominate a new trump suit, as long as it is higher-ranking than the trump suit of his winning bid.

▶ **FOUR-HANDED PREFERENCE**
- Preference can be played with four participants instead of the usual three. When four players are involved, the dealer sits out of the game for the duration of his deal.
- Because the dealership rotates, each player is required to sit out in turn while the previous dealer has a chance to play. Enough deals should be played for every player to sit out an equal number of times.
- All other rules remain the same.

Skat

Skat is regarded as one of the most taxing and rewarding card games for three players. It was invented in the town of Altenburg in eastern Germany around the year 1810. Skat is the best-known card game in Germany and is played throughout the world both socially and in tournaments.

Objective

Players attempt to win the right to choose the game to be played and then try to complete that game.

Card values

- All cards with a face value below seven are removed from a standard deck to leave a playing deck of 32 cards.
- When no trumps are in play, Aces are the highest-ranking cards, followed by Kings, Queens, Jacks, tens, nines, eights and sevens respectively.
- Jacks are always the top-ranking trumps (when trumps are in play) and are themselves ranked with J♣ the highest, followed by J♠ then J♥ and J♦ the lowest. Tens rank above Kings when trumps are in play.

▼ Suit ranking with no trumps

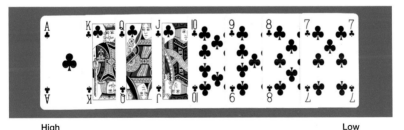

High   Low

▼ Suit ranking with spades as trumps

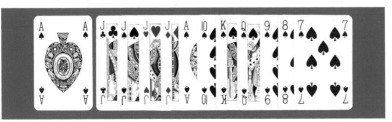

Trump   High   Low

▶ Suit
ranking of
all other
suits with
spades as
trumps

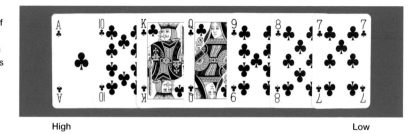

High   Low

CARD VALUES

In games with trumps, the cards have the following point values:

Card	Points
Jack	2
Ace	11
Ten	10
King	4
Queen	3
Nine, eight and seven	0

Dealing

● The first dealer is chosen at random or by mutual consent and the dealership subsequently passes in a clockwise direction. The cards are shuffled by the player to the dealer's right and then cut by the player to the dealer's left before the deal is made.

● A packet of three cards is dealt to each player followed by two cards to the centre of the table. These two cards are known as the 'Skat'. Each player then receives a packet of four cards followed by another packet of three cards. All cards are dealt face-down.

Bidding

● Players make bids that equal the point values of possible games. By making a bid, a player undertakes to win at least that number of points in the subsequent trick-winning phase of the game. The calculation of point values for possible games is explained in Game values (see page 122).

● Traditionally, the three players in a game of Skat are known as 'forehand', 'middlehand' and 'rearhand'. Forehand is the player to the dealer's left, middlehand is the player to forehand's left, and rearhand is the player to middlehand's left (in other words, the dealer).

● The first round of bidding takes place between forehand and middlehand, with middlehand having the first bid or pass.

- If middlehand makes a bid, forehand may either pass or say 'yes', which means that he accepts the number of points bid. Middlehand may then pass or make a higher bid, which forehand can again pass or accept. The process continues until a player passes.
- Bidding is now conducted between rearhand and the winner of the first bidding round (either forehand or middlehand). Rearhand may pass or make a bid higher than the last bid made in the first round of bidding which middlehand may pass or accept. Bidding continues until one player passes.
- The player who made the last bid is known as the 'declarer' and wins the bidding phase with the last bid he made or accepted.
- If middlehand and rearhand pass without making a bid, forehand may become the declarer at the lowest possible bid (See Game values, page 122) or can cause the hand to be abandoned by declining the bid. In this case, a new deal is made by the next dealer.

EXAMPLE OF PLAY

Example of possible bidding:

Forehand	Middlehand	Rearhand
	18	
YES	20	
YES	PASS	
YES		22
YES		23
YES		PASS

1 Middlehand opens the bidding with 18 (the lowest possible bid).
2 Forehand accepts the bid by calling 'yes'.
3 Middlehand has the option to pass, leaving forehand with a bid of 18, but decides to raise the bid to 20 instead.
4 Forehand accepts the raised bid by calling 'yes'.
5 Middlehand passes.
6 Forehand has won the first stage of the bidding with a bid of 20 and goes on to bid against rearhand.
7 Rearhand bids 22 (his bid must be higher than the highest bid made or accepted in the first stage).
8 Forehand accepts the raised bid.
9 Rearhand raises the bid to 23.
10 Forehand accepts the raised bid.
11 Rearhand passes. Forehand wins the bidding with a bid of 23.

The games

- The player who wins the bidding has the right to name the game that will be played (to declare the game).
- The winning bidder also has the right to look at the two cards dealt face-down on the table (the Skat) if he chooses.
- The declarer may pick up the Skat and discard any two cards from his hand, face-down, including either or both of the Skat cards. Any cards discarded at this point count towards the declarer's final score.
- Alternatively, the declarer may decide to play 'from the hand' without picking up the Skat. In this case, no player may look at the Skat during the course of the deal.
- For the purposes of calculating the value of a game (see Game values, page 122) the Skat is counted as part of the declarer's hand.
- If the declarer has picked up the Skat, any game he declares is known as a 'Skat game'. If he does not, any game declared is a 'hand game'.
- The declarer may declare any of the four games described in the following table:

GAMES

Suit games (Diamonds Hearts Spades Clubs)	The named suit is trumps and the declarer undertakes to collect at least 61 card points.
Grand	Jacks are the only trumps and the declarer undertakes to collect at least 61 card points.
Null	There are no trumps and the declarer undertakes to lose every trick.
Null ouvert (or open null)	There are no trumps and the declarer undertakes to lose every trick with his cards turned face-up.

- For suit hand games or grand hand games, the declarer may also call 'schneider', which is an undertaking on his part to collect at least 90 card points, or 'schwarz', which is an undertaking to win all tricks, or 'open' which is an undertaking to win all the tricks in the deal with his cards turned face-up.
- These additional calls can only be made for hand games (games in which the declarer has not looked at the Skat) and must be made before the first trick is lead.

Playing

- Forehand always leads the first trick, regardless of which player is declarer, and play passes in a clockwise direction. To lead the trick, forehand must place any card face-up on the table. The suit of that card is known as the 'lead' suit for that trick.
- The next player must play a card of the lead suit if he has one. If he has no cards of the lead suit he may play any other card from his hand, including trump cards.
- In any game where trumps are in play (suit and grand games) Jacks are considered to be part of the trump suit only. For example, in a game where spades are trumps, the Jack of hearts, the Jack of diamonds and the Jack of clubs can only be played as trump cards; they cannot be played to follow the lead suit if that is hearts, diamonds or clubs.
- The trick ends once all three players have contributed one card. If no trump cards have been played, the winner of the trick is the player who contributed the highest-ranking card of the lead suit. If trump cards have been played, the trick is won by the highest-ranking trump. The winner of a trick leads the next trick.

EXAMPLES OF PLAY

Example 1 of possible trick play:
1   The game is a diamonds Skat game, which means that the declarer has looked at the Skat and diamonds are trumps.
2   Forehand leads, because it is the first trick of the match, and plays 10♠. Spades is the lead suit for the trick.
3   Middlehand follows the lead suit with K♠.
4   Rearhand also follows the lead suit with 8♠.
5   Forehand wins the trick because his was the highest-ranking card played of the lead suit (tens rank higher than Kings) and no trumps were played.

Example 2 of possible trick play:
1   The game is a grand Skat game, which means that the declarer has looked at the Skat and only the four Jacks are trumps.
2   Middlehand (hypothetically the winner of the last trick) leads with 8♦. Diamonds are the lead suit for the trick.
3   Rearhand has no cards of the lead suit and plays J♥, a trump card.
4   Forehand has no cards of the lead suit and no trump cards. He plays 7♠.
5   Rearhand wins the trick. His trump card outranks the only card played in the lead suit, middlehand's 8♦.

Game values

● Bids made in the bidding phase are predictions of the number of points that a player will win in a game (the value of a game).

● The value of a game is calculated by multiplying the 'base value' by the 'multiplier'.

BASE VALUES

Trump suit	Base value
Diamonds	9
Hearts	10
Spades	11
Clubs	12
Grand (Jacks)	24

The multiplier is the sum of the applicable points from the following table:

MULTIPLIERS

Multiplier	Skat game	Hand game
Matadors (with or against)	1 for each	1 for each
Game (always applies)	1	1
Hand game	n/a	1
Schneider (90 or more card points to one side)	1	1
Announced schneider	n/a	1
Schwarz (all tricks won by one side)	1	1
Announced schwarz	n/a	1
Open	n/a	1

Matadors

● The Jack of clubs plus any unbroken sequence of trumps following it in a player's hand are known as 'matadors'.

● If the declarer has such a sequence, he is said to be 'with (number) matador(s)'. If such a sequence is to be found in the combined hands of the declarer's opponents, he is said to be 'against (number) matador(s)'.

● The number of matadors with or against a declarer is the number of trump cards present in an unbroken sequence, along with the Jack of clubs, in the relevant hand or hands.

Examples of matador count with spades as trumps:

Declarer's cards include	Declarer is
(J♣, J♠ J♥) A♠, 10♠, Q♠, 8♠	with 3 matadors

Brackets indicate the unbroken sequences of matadors. In this case there are three, J♦ is missing, so the declarer is with 3 matadors and the multiplier is 3.

Declarer's cards include	Declarer is
(J♣) J♥, J♦, A♦, 10♦, K♦	with 1 matador

Brackets indicate the unbroken sequence of matadors. In this case there is only one, so the declarer is with 1 matador and the multiplier is 1.

Declarer's cards include	Declarer is
J♥, J♦, A♦, 10♦, K♦, 7♥ A♥	against 2 matadors

The top two trumps, J♣ and J♠, are missing so they must be in the hands of the declarer's opponents. Declarer is against 2 matadors and the multiplier is 2.

- Because the Jack of clubs must always be in either the declarer's hand or the hand of one of his opponents, the declarer will always be with or against at least one matador. Therefore, the multiplier will always be at least one.
- The game multiplier always applies as well, since one side or other must have won the game. Consequently, there will always be a multiplier of at least two (one matador plus one game).
- Since the lowest base value is nine (for a game with diamonds as trumps) the lowest possible game value is eighteen (nine multiplied by two). Eighteen is, therefore, the lowest possible bid.
- When calculating the value of a game, all applicable multipliers must be included. For example, if a declarer wins a suit game and has announced schneider, the applicable multipliers would be: Game (always applies), Matadors (always applies), Hand (announced schneider is only legal in hand games), Schneider (the declarer collected 90 or more points), Schneider announced (the declarer announced his schneider).

▼ A 19th-century English Queen of spades

● An open suit or open grand game would include all of the multipliers, because both schneider and schwarz are implicit in a bid to win all tricks, and because both have effectively been announced by declaring an open game.

Null games

● Null game values are fixed, the base values and multipliers used to calculate the value of suit and grand games do not apply. Null game values are as follows:

NULL GAME VALUES

Game	Value
Null Skat	23
Null hand	35
Null Skat open	46
Null hand open	59

Scoring

● Only the declarer of a game gains or loses points at the end of that game. Points are not awarded to or subtracted from opponents.

● A declarer who wins his game receives the same number of points as the value of the game, as long as that value is equal to or greater than the declarer's bid.

● A declarer who loses his game loses points equal to double the value of the game, as long as that value is less than the declarer's bid.

● A declarer automatically loses a game if the value of the game is less than his bid, regardless of the number of card points collected. In this case, the declarer loses points equal to twice the lowest multiplier of the base value of the game played that would have fulfilled the bid.

● A declarer who has announced schneider but collects less than 90 card points, or who has announced schwarz or open and loses one trick, automatically loses the game. Points equal to twice the value of the game, including all multipliers that would have applied had the declarer won, are subtracted from the declarer's total.

● Sessions usually continue until all players have had the opportunity to deal an equal number of times.

● Cumulative scores for all players are recorded throughout a playing session. This may be done by any player.

● The player with the highest score at the end of the session wins.

Skat variants

▶ **FOUR- AND FIVE-HANDED SKAT**

● Skat is often played with four or five players. Only three players actually play during a deal. The dealer sits out in games with four players and the dealer and the fifth player sit out in games with five. Because the dealership rotates, all players have a chance to participate over the course of an entire game.

● With four or more players, the player to the dealer's left is known as 'forehand', the next player as 'middlehand', and the next player as 'endhand'. As the dealership passes to the left, each player has the chance to play as forehand, middlehand and endhand in turn.

● All other rules remain the same.

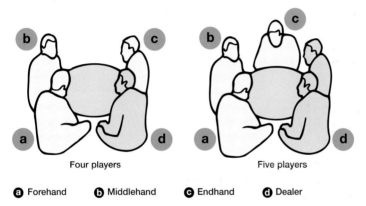

Four players   Five players

ⓐ Forehand   ⓑ Middlehand   ⓒ Endhand   ⓓ Dealer

▼ Cards from a French deck of the revolutionary period depicting Classical heroes and revolutionary symbols

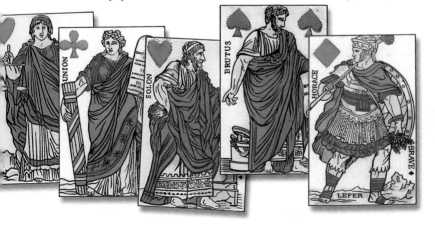

games

for four

Card games for four are often played in double partnerships, with all the tactical challenges such an arrangement brings. Many of the world's most taxing and most popular card games are four-player doubles games.

Canasta

Canasta originated in Uruguay around 1940 and quickly spread to the rest of South, and then North, America. The rules for Classic canasta were standardised in the United States in the 1950s. The game became extremely popular and, for a time, seemed set to supplant Contract bridge as the world's favourite.

Objective

To win the largest number of points by melding all the cards in your hand with your partner's cards before the opposition.

Card values

● Canasta is played with a deck of 108 cards: two fifty-two card decks plus four Jokers. The point values for each card are as follows:

POINT VALUES FOR CARDS

Card	Points
Joker	50
Ace and 2	20
King, Queen, Jack, 10, 9, 8,	10
7, 6, 5, 4	5

● The cards Ace, King, Queen, Jack, ten, nine, eight, seven, six, five and four are known as the natural cards.

● Twos and Jokers are wild cards and may be substituted for any natural card in most instances.

● Threes have special functions and point values explained later.

Partnerships and dealing

● Partnerships are decided randomly or by mutual consent, as is the first dealer. The deal passes clockwise to the next player on the left at the end of each hand.

● The player to the left of the dealer shuffles the cards, and the player to the right shuffles them before the deal is made.

● Each player receives eleven cards dealt face-down and one at a time.

- The rest of the cards are placed face-down in the centre of the table as the 'stock'.
- The top card of the stock is placed, face-up, next to the stock to start the discard pile.
- The top card of the discard pile must be a natural card at this stage of the game. If the first card is a wild card, or a red three (heart or diamond), another card from the stock must be placed on top of it.
- Players must immediately place any red threes they have been dealt face-up on the table in front of them and replace them with an equal number of cards from the stock.

Melds

- Achieving melds is the main element of play in Canasta. There are several rules that restrict the formation of melds.
- A meld consists of three or more cards with the same face value.
- Every meld must contain at least two natural cards. The smallest melds must, therefore, consist of three natural cards of the same face value, or two natural cards of the same face value and a wild card.
- A meld may not contain more than three wild cards.
- A meld of seven cards is known as a canasta. Since no meld may contain more than three wild cards, a canasta will always contain at least four natural cards. A partnership must achieve at least one canasta before a member of that partnership can legally get rid of all of his cards and end the game.
- There is no legal limit to the size of a meld, but it may never contain more than three wild cards. Logically, since there are only eight cards of any one face value in the deck, the largest possible meld would contain eleven cards.
- A meld with no wild cards is known as 'natural', a meld with wild cards is known as a 'mixed meld'. The same terms apply to canastas.

Playing

- Play begins with the player to the left of the dealer and passes in a clockwise direction. Partners should sit so that play alternates between one team and the other.
- To start his turn a player must pick up the top card from the stock. Alternatively he may, under certain conditions, pick the entire discard pile up.
- The player may then meld, if he has the opportunity. Melding is not compulsory.

● To end a turn, a player must discard one card face-up on the discard pile. A player may not discard his last card if his partnership has not made a canasta. To avoid this, a player must play in such a way that he is able to discard at the end of his turn while still retaining at least one card. A player cannot avoid discarding.

● A player may pick up the entire discard pile if he is able to use the top card of the pile with at least two other cards from his hand (natural or wild) to form a meld.

● To pick up the discard pile, a player places the two or more cards from his hand that will be used in the meld face-up on the table. He adds the top card from the discard pile to form the meld and adds the rest of the discard pile to his hand. He may then form further melds before finally discarding a card to end his turn.

Freezing

● The discard pile is not always available to a partnership. It may be 'frozen' (not available) under three circumstances:

1) The discard pile is frozen to all players if it contains a wild card. When a wild card is placed on the discard pile, it is positioned at 90 degrees to the other cards so that it remains visible after subsequent discards have been placed on top of it.

2) The discard pile is frozen to all players if the first card from the stock was a red three. A red three is positioned in the same way as a wild card so that it remains visible.

3) The discard pile is frozen to a partnership until it makes its first meld.

● A player may only take the discard pile when it is frozen if he can form a meld with the top card and at least two natural cards (not wild cards) from his hand.

Meld requirements

● A partnership may only lay down its first meld if it has a minimum point value. This value depends on the partnership's cumulative score from previous hands.

● The initial meld requirements may be met by laying down more than one meld at once.

● The discard pile is frozen before a partnership's initial meld, so the first meld must come from the hand plus whatever is drawn from the stock, or the requirements for taking the frozen discard pile must be met. When making an initial meld from the discard pile, only the top card of the pile counts towards the point value of that meld.

Cumulative score	Minimum point value of initial meld
Negative	15
0 – 1495	50
1500 – 2995	90
3000 plus	120

Meld requirements

● Any red threes that a player may have put down before making an initial meld do not count towards the initial meld score. Even a full canasta may not be put down if it does not meet the score required.

● The only exception to the initial meld requirements is when a player, having drawn from the stock, is able to meld all of his cards, including a canasta, with or without making a discard.

Threes

● The following rules apply to red threes:

1) A player dealt a red three must immediately place it face-up on the table and draw a replacement card from the stock. Bonuses are awarded at the end of a deal for these threes.

2) If a red three is turned up as the first card of the discard pile it is turned 90 degrees so that it remains visible and another card from the stock is placed on top of it. The player who takes a discard pile frozen in this way immediately places the red three face-up on the table, but does not draw a replacement for it.

● The following rules apply to black threes:

1) Discarding a black three prevents the next player from taking the discard pile. This effect only lasts until a subsequent card is discarded on top of the black three (at the end of the next player's turn).

2) Black threes may not be melded unless a player is going out. In this case a player may meld three or four black threes but black-three melds must not include wild cards.

◀ A 19th-century French card depicting Queen Victoria

Ending play

- A player who legally gets rid of all his cards is said to have 'gone out'.
- A deal ends when the first player goes out.
- A player who goes out by laying down his entire hand, including a canasta, without having previously made any melds is said to have 'gone out concealed' which earns a points bonus.
- A player can only go out if his partnership has achieved at least one canasta. Forming the canasta may be part of a player's last turn.
- After drawing from the stock, but before going out, a player has the option of asking his partner 'may I go out?'. He must then comply with his partner's answer of 'yes' or 'no'. It is not compulsory to ask a partner's permission to go out.
- A deal also ends if there are no more cards left in the stock at the point where a player is required to draw one.

Scoring

- As soon as play has ended, each partnership scores its hand. This score consists of:

    1) The total value of all of the cards they have melded (see Point values for cards, page 128).

    2) Minus the total value of any cards remaining in the hand.

    3) Plus the total of any bonuses (see Canasta bonuses below).

- Cumulative scores are kept for both partnerships. The first side to reach 5000 points wins the game.

CANASTA BONUSES

Bonus	Points
Going out	100
Going out concealed (in addition to going out bonus)	100
Each natural canasta	500
Each mixed canasta	300
Each red three* (if team has at least one meld)	100
All red threes** (in addition to individual red three bonuses)	400

*Red threes score -100 points if no meld

**All red threes score additional -400 if no meld

▲ A 19th-century card depicting George Washington

CANASTA

Strategy tips

● It is rarely an advantage to go out as quickly as possible. The more cards you can collect in your hand, the more opportunities you have for forming canastas and the more points you will have the opportunity to win.

● It is almost always a good idea to take a large discard pile if you are able. It gives you many more cards to form melds with and denies their use to the opposition.

● Small discard piles are rarely worth taking because the opposition will remember most of the cards in the pile and know what you have.

● Do not meld wild cards if you have the corresponding natural cards. Always save wild cards as long as possible.

● You do not have to meld everything in your hand. For example, if you have five kings, you can meld three of them and keep the other two hidden in your hand in case you need them later to take a frozen discard pile.

● Black threes are valuable cards because they can always be discarded without the risk of giving the opposition a card they need.

● If your opponents secure control of a large discard pile try to go out as quickly as you can in order to minimise the points they can gain.

▲ A 19th-century English five of spades depicting a circus acrobat

Canasta variants

▶ **FROZEN DISCARD PILE**

● The discard pile is always frozen. Wild cards and red threes have no effect on the discard pile.

▶ **WILD CARD MELDS**

● Melds consisting entirely of wild cards are allowed.

● A canasta consisting entirely of wild cards is known as a 'wild canasta' and carries a bonus of 1000 points.

● Wild canastas consisting entirely of twos, or containing all four Jokers, may be given additional bonuses.

● When wild canastas are allowed, a partnership is usually not allowed to use wild cards in any other meld until the wild canasta is completed.

▶ **MODERN AMERICAN CANASTA**

● Modern American canasta, played in the United States, has entirely different rules to Classic canasta.

▶ # Contract bridge

NUMBER OF CARDS

52

One deck of 52 cards

RANKING ORDER

high

low

Bridge is one of the world's most popular card games. Contract bridge, the most common form of Bridge, was invented in the 1920s, but the game has its roots in Whist, which is at least 400 years old. Bridge is one of the few card games that has 'official' sets of rules drawn up by the governing bodies of the various international Bridge associations. The version of Contract bridge given here is suitable for home players.

Objective

To win the largest number of points during the course of three games, known as a 'rubber'. Points are won by accurately predicting the number of tricks that you and your partner can win in each game.

Card values

● Contract bridge is played with a single standard deck of 52 cards. The cards rank in their suits with Aces highest, followed by Kings, Queens, Jacks, tens, nines, eights, sevens, sixes, fives, fours, threes and twos (lowest).

● The four suits also have a fixed rank. Spades are the highest-ranking suit, hearts second, diamonds third and clubs the lowest.

● When two cards have the same face value, the suit ranks are used to determine which is the higher-ranking card.

▼ Suit ranking

Highest   Lowest

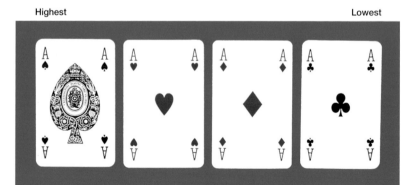

Partnerships and dealing

● Partnerships must be decided before hands can be dealt.

● The four players must be divided into two partnerships. Traditionally, players are referred to as occupying compass directions. North always partners with South, and East with West. The diagram below shows the partnership seating positions.

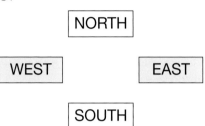

● Partnerships are decided by each player drawing a card from the face-down deck. The two players with the highest-ranking cards become one partnership, while the other two players form the other partnership. The player with the highest-ranking card overall has the choice of seats, and therefore determines the positions of the other three.

EXAMPLE OF PLAY

Example of possible play when deciding partnerships:

1   Players A, B, C and D draw 7♠, 7♥, 9♦, 4♣ respectively.
2   Player C has drawn the highest card (9♦) and D has the lowest (4♣). Player A's 7♠ ranks higher that B's 7♥ because spades rank higher than hearts. Therefore, A partners C, and B partners D.
3   If C, as the player with the highest draw, elects to sit in the North position, A will be South, and B and D may occupy East and West as they choose.

● The player who made the highest draw becomes the first dealer.

● Before dealing, the player to the dealer's left shuffles the cards, then the player to the dealer's right cuts them.

● Thirteen cards are dealt, face-down and one at a time, to each player starting with the player to the dealer's left and continuing clockwise. There are no cards left over.

● Traditionally, the dealer's partner shuffles a second deck of cards while the deal is taking place so that the next dealer will have a shuffled deck ready for use. This is just to save time: the game can be played with only one deck.

Playing

- Play consists of two phases: bidding and trick-taking play.
- The number of tricks that each partnership must win in order to gain maximum points is determined during bidding. Bidding takes place first.
- During play, each partnership attempts to fulfil its bidding commitment.
- Even though bidding takes place first, it is necessary to understand the basics of how tricks are won before learning about bidding.

Winning tricks

- The lead player (determined in the bidding phase) may play any card from the hand by placing it face-up on the table. The suit of that card is known as the 'lead' suit for that trick.
- Each player in turn, proceeding clockwise from the leader, must place one card face-up on the table.
- A player must play a card of the same suit as the leader if they have one. Cards of any other suit may only be played if there is no leading-suit card available.
- The card with the highest face value from the leading suit wins the trick. The suit ranks are not relevant in this phase of the game.

EXAMPLE OF PLAY

Example of possible play in the trick-winning phase:
1. North leads with J♠, so spades is the lead suit. Play passes clockwise to East.
2. East follows the lead suit and plays 9♠.
3. South also follows suit and plays A♠.
4. West has no spades and plays A♥.
5. South's A♠ wins the trick because it was the highest-ranking card played in the leading suit.

North	East	South	West

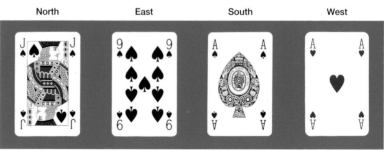

Leads

Trumps

- During the bidding phase, a particular suit may be designated as trumps. During trick play, a trump outranks any card of a different suit, including the lead suit.
- A player who cannot follow suit does not have to play a trump card even if one is available.

EXAMPLE OF PLAY

Example of possible play in the trick-winning phase with clubs as the trump suit:

1 North leads with 7 ♥.
2 East follows the lead suit and plays 9 ♥.
3 South also follows the lead suit and plays 3 ♥.
4 West has no hearts, and is therefore allowed to play the trump suit card 7 ♣, instead.
5 West's trump wins the trick, even though East's card has a higher face value and belongs to the leading suit.

North	East	South	West

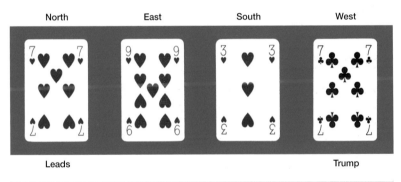

| Leads | | | Trump |

Bidding

- Bidding takes place after partnerships have been decided and the deal has been made.
- During bidding, partnerships compete for the right to name the trump suit for that deal (or no trumps) by committing themselves to winning more tricks than their opponents.
- Since each player has thirteen cards, and plays one card per trick, there are always thirteen tricks in a deal.
- The partnership that bids the highest number of tricks stands to win the largest number of points if it achieves that goal, but the higher the bid, the more difficult it is to achieve.

● The first six tricks in a deal are known as 'the book', and are not counted as part of the bidding. A player may bid between one and seven tricks. A bid of 'one diamond', commits the partnership to winning six tricks (the book) plus one more trick, with diamonds as trumps. A bid of 'seven hearts', commits the partnership to winning all the tricks in the deal (the book plus seven more tricks, totalling thirteen tricks) with hearts as trumps.

● The dealer makes the first bid. Bidding continues clockwise around the table until three players in a row pass.

● Every player has the right to make a bid or pass, but a bid must be higher than any previous bid made by another player. This means that a bid must commit the partnership to taking a higher number of tricks, or taking the same or a higher number of tricks in a higher-ranking suit.

● A player may also bid 'no trumps' rather than naming a particular suit as trumps. A bid of 'three no trumps' would therefore commit the partnership to winning nine tricks (the book plus three more), with no trump suit in

EXAMPLES OF PLAY

Example 1 of possible play during the bidding phase:

WEST	NORTH	EAST	SOUTH
PASS	1 ♦	1 ♥	3 ♣
PASS	3 ♠	PASS	3 NO TRUMP
PASS	PASS	PASS	

1   West opens the bidding phase with a pass. Play passes clockwise to North.
2   North bids 1 ♦, committing the North-South partnership to taking seven tricks (the book plus one more) with diamonds as trumps.
3   East bids 1 ♥. The East-West partnership commits to the same number of tricks as North-South, but this is a legal bid because hearts rank higher than diamonds.
4   South bids 3 ♣. Clubs rank lower than hearts, but the commitment to taking nine tricks still makes this a higher bid than East's.
5   West passes again.
6   North bids 3 ♠. Spades outrank the clubs bid by South.
7   East passes.
8   South bids 3 no trump. No trump outranks any of the suits.
9   West, North and East pass, so the bidding ends. South, the last to bid, has won the bidding by committing North-South to taking nine tricks with no trumps.

operation. In no trump tricks, the lead suit has the highest rank.

● For bidding purposes, the highest-ranking is no trumps, followed by spades, hearts, diamonds and, lowest-ranking, clubs. These five bidding options (the four suits plus no trumps) are known as the bidding strains.

● The ranking of the strains is reflected in the points awarded for winning tricks. A trick won under no trumps brings more points than a trick won under the lower-ranking diamonds.

● If the first three players in the bidding phase pass, the fourth player may still bid. If the fourth player also passes, the deal is abandoned and a new deal is made by the next dealer.

● Bidding ends when three players pass in a row. The last bid made before the three passes becomes the winning bid and is known as the contract (hence the name Contract bridge).

Example 2 of possible play during the bidding phase:

EAST	SOUTH	WEST	NORTH
1 ♥	PASS	2 ♥	2 ♠
3 ♦	PASS	PASS	PASS

◀ A French card from the time of the Revolution

1 East opens the bidding with a bid of 1 ♥.

2 South passes.

3 West raises the bidding to 2 ♥.

4 North raises the bidding again to 2 ♠ (spades outrank hearts).

5 East raises the bidding to 3 ♦ (diamonds rank lower than spades, but the bid of three tricks makes this a higher bid).

6 South, West and North pass. East's bid of 3 ♦ wins the bidding phase and commits East-West to taking nine tricks with diamonds as trumps.

VENDANGEUR

Declarer and dummy

● Once a partnership has won the bidding phase, only one player from that partnership plays during the trick-taking phase.

● The playing partner is known as the 'declarer', and the other partner is known as the 'dummy'.

● At the beginning of the trick-taking phase, the dummy turns his cards face-up on the table. The declarer plays his own cards and the dummy's cards, still in the correct order of play, as if he had a second hand of cards.

● The declarer is the member of the winning partnership in the bidding phase who first named the strain of the winning bid.

EXAMPLES OF PLAY

Example 1 of possible play during the bidding phase:

WEST	NORTH	EAST	SOUTH
PASS	1♠	PASS	2♠
PASS	PASS	PASS	

1 North-South win the bidding phase with a contract to take eight tricks with spades as trumps.

2 North, as the first to bid spades, becomes the declarer and South is the dummy.

Example 2 of possible play during bidding:

SOUTH	WEST	NORTH	EAST
PASS	1♥	2♣	2♦
PASS	3♦	PASS	3♥
PASS	4♥	PASS	
PASS			

1 East-West win the bidding with a contract to take ten tricks with hearts as trumps.

2 Even though West bid 3♦ at one point, he was the first to bid hearts, which was the winning strain.

3 The fact that other players bid other suits, and the fact that East was also the last to bid hearts is irrelevant. East was the first member of the winning partnership to bid hearts, so East is declarer and West is the dummy.

Double and redouble

● During bidding a player may 'double' or 'redouble' a previous player's bid, as long as that player was an opponent and no other bids have been made since then.

● A successful double bid increases the number of points that can be scored in a deal.

● Fulfilling a doubled contract greatly increases the number of points to be won, but also the penalty that will go to the opposition if the contract is not fulfilled.

EXAMPLE OF PLAY

Example of possible play during the bidding phase:

▲ A Chinese playing card

NORTH	EAST	SOUTH	WEST
PASS	1 ♦	PASS	1 ♥
PASS	2 ♦	PASS	PASS
DOUBLE	3 ♦	PASS	PASS
PASS			

1 North leads with a pass.
2 East bids 1 ♦, South passes and West bids 1 ♥.
3 North wishes to double 1 ♦, but cannot because it was not the last bid made before his turn (West's 1 ♥ was the last bid made), so he passes.
4 East raises the bid to 2 ♦.
5 South and West pass. North may now double the 2 ♦ since it was the last bid made before his turn.
6 Three passes follow North's bid. North-South have made a contract of double 2 ♦ (8 tricks with diamonds as trumps and bonus points available). North is the declarer and South the dummy.

● A player may redouble if the last bid made by an opponent was a double and there have been no intervening bids.

● A redouble increases the potential rewards of fulfilling the contract, as well as the potential penalties for failing.

● Doubles and redoubles are cancelled if any player makes another bid after they have been called. In other words, a double or redouble bid only stands if it is followed by three passes.

● Redoubles cannot themselves be redoubled. A bid may only be played, doubled, redoubled or cancelled by a subsequent bid.

EXAMPLE OF PLAY

Example of possible play during the bidding phase:

NORTH	EAST	SOUTH	WEST
1♠	DOUBLE	PASS	2♦
2♠	DOUBLE	REDOUBLE	3♦
PASS	PASS	PASS	PASS
PASS	PASS	3♠	

1 North leads with a bid of 1♠ which is doubled by his opponent East.
2 South passes and West cancels East's double by making a new bid of 2♦.
3 North raises the bid to 2♠, which East doubles.
4 South redoubles his opponent, East's, double.
5 West cancels the redouble with a new bid of 3♦.
6 North and East pass. South raises the bid to 3♠.
7 The final contract is the bid of 3♠ made by North-South. North is the declarer and South the dummy.

Rubbers

● The essential unit of play in bridge is the rubber. To win a rubber, a partnership must win two games (a bonus is also awarded for this). To win a game, a partnership must accumulate 100 points. Points are awarded for each trick won.

● Games may be won in just one deal (thirteen tricks) or it may take more than one deal for a partnership to accumulate enough points.

Starting play

● Once the bidding phase is over and a contract has been made, the trick-taking phase begins.

● Play begins with the player to the left of the declarer and proceeds in a clockwise direction.

▲ A 19th-century Austrian four of clubs

● Next in sequence is the dummy, whose face-up hand is played by the declarer. The player to the left of the dummy is next, then the declarer plays from his own hand (known as the closed hand) to complete the trick.

● The winner of the trick leads the next. If the winning card was played from the dummy's hand by the declarer, the declarer must play the next lead from that hand; he may not play from his own.

Scoring

● Scoring in bridge is a complex process that has a strong bearing on the strategy of game play.

● The score sheet is divided into two columns, one for each partnership, headed 'We' and 'They'. The score keeper enters points for his own team under the 'We' column and points for the opposing partnership under the 'They' column. Some players prefer to have one member of each team keeping score to avoid discrepancies.

● The horizontal line on the score sheet is important. Only points that are entered below the line count towards winning a game.

● When scoring, only tricks won in excess of the book (the first six tricks) are awarded points. These are known as 'odd tricks' and their scores are entered below the line. Points for tricks are shown in the table below:

▶ Sample Bridge score sheet

POINT VALUES FOR TRICKS

Contract strain	Score per odd trick
No trumps	40 (first trick) 30 (other tricks)
Spades or hearts	30
Diamonds or clubs	20

EXAMPLE OF PLAY

Example of possible odd trick scoring:

1 You are scoring, so points scored by your partnership are entered under 'We'.

2 You fulfil a contract of 2♠. Enter 60 points (2 odd tricks at 30 points each). These points are recorded below the line and therefore go towards winning a game.

3 The opposition scores nothing.

WE	THEY
60	

Overtricks and undertricks

● If a partnership wins more tricks than it had contracted to, the extra tricks are known as 'overtricks'. If it wins fewer, the missing tricks are known as 'undertricks'.

● Bonus points are awarded for overtricks and penalty points are awarded to the opposition for undertricks.

● Bonus points and penalty points are recorded above the horizontal line on the score sheet; they do not count towards winning games.

Vulnerability

● A partnership is said to be 'vulnerable' if it has won a game and 'not vulnerable' if it has not. Vulnerability affects the scale of penalty points. A vulnerable partnership is liable to suffer higher penalty awards to the opposition than a non-vulnerable partnership.

PENALTY POINT VALUES FOR UNDERTRICKS

Vulnerability	Score per undertrick
Not vulnerable	50
Doubled	100 (1st trick) 200 (2nd and 3rd trick) 300 (4th trick plus)
Redoubled	200 (1st trick) 400 (2nd and 3rd trick) 600 (4th trick plus)
Vulnerable	100
Doubled	200 (1st trick) 300 (additional tricks)
Redoubled	400 (1st trick) 600 (additional tricks)

EXAMPLE OF PLAY

Example of possible overtrick scoring:

1 Your partnership bids two no trumps but takes ten tricks.

2 You receive 70 points below the line (40 for the first odd trick and 30 for the second) and 60 above the line (30 each for the two overtricks).

3 A bid of three no trumps would have won you a game.

WE	THEY
60	
70	

EXAMPLE OF PLAY

Example of possible penalty scoring:

1 Your partnership bids 4 hearts and takes 11 tricks.
2 You score 120 points below the line and 30 above.
3 Because you have won a game (you have more than 100 points below the line) a new horizontal line is drawn below your score. You are now vulnerable.
4 For the next deal you bid 3 spades, but only capture seven tricks.
5 Your opponents score 200 above the line (two undertricks at 100 points each).
6 For the next deal you bid 3 diamonds and your opponents' double, but you only capture six tricks (you are still vulnerable).
7 Your opponents score 800 points above the line (200 for the first undertrick and 300 each for the other two).

WE	THEY
	800
30	200
120	

Other bonuses

● Winning a rubber (two games) brings a rubber bonus of 700 points, if the winners' opponents have not won a game; or 500 points, if the winners' opponents have won a game.

● Bonus points are also awarded to any player (declaring or defending) holding honour cards. The honour cards are the Ace, King, Queen, Jack and ten in the trump suit. 100 points are awarded for holding any four honour cards and 150 points for holding all five.

● Taking 12 tricks is known as a 'small slam' and earns 500 points for a non-vulnerable pair or 750 points for a vulnerable pair. Taking all thirteen tricks is known as a 'grand slam' and earns 1000 points for a non-vulnerable pair or 1500 points for a vulnerable pair.

● These bonuses are unaffected by doubles or redoubles. Bonus points are recorded above the line on the score sheet.

▼ A 19th-century Jack of hearts

Strategy tips

- There are strict rules in tournament bridge games governing communication between players. These are known as the proprieties. Knowing exactly which cards your partner is holding would be an enormous advantage, especially during the bidding phase. Rules exist to prevent this.
- Essentially, the proprieties say that the only communication that may take place between partners is through the plays that are made and the use of the correct calls. Non-standard wording of calls, hesitation, emphasis, facial expression or any other means of communication are illegal.
- During the bidding phase, the only legal calls are 'pass', 'double', 'redouble' or a bid in the form 'number, strain' (for example '3 diamonds'). No other wording, such as 'I bid 3 diamonds' or 'I pass', may be used.
- Players are not allowed to communicate hesitation or eagerness over a play by varying the speed of their actions. You may not, for example, indicate to your partner that you have many cards of a certain suit by excitedly doubling an opponent's bid in that suit.
- Most challenging of all is the rule that forbids you from making inferences from your partner's behaviour. In other words, even if your partner is acting illegally and, intentionally or otherwise, giving you information, you must play as if you did not have that information.
- Clearly, home games do not have to be played under such strict conditions, but the proprieties do add to the challenge and interest of the game by forcing players to think more carefully about tactics. As in all card games, it is a player's uncertainty about the location of cards that constitutes the game.

Bridge variants

▶ **AUCTION BRIDGE**
- Auction bridge represents an intermediary stage of evolution between Whist, the ancestor of Bridge, and Contract bridge.
- The rules of play are the same as for Contract bridge, but scoring is different, which affects players' strategies.

Scoring tricks
- Vulnerability does not exist, so there is no additional penalty for failing to fulfil a contract when one side has already won a deal.
- Odd tricks are scored below the line whether they were contracted for or not, and count towards winning a deal if the declarer has at least fulfilled the contract.

Points are as follows:

Points for tricks won	♣	♦	♥	♠	NT
Undoubled	6	7	8	9	10
Doubled	12	14	16	18	20
Redoubled	24	28	32	36	40

Scoring honours
● Three or more honours in the trump suit, or three or more Aces in no trumps, earn above-the-line points for the partnership that holds them as follows:

Honours	Points
Three honours (or Aces)	30
Four honours (or Aces) divided	40
Five honours divided	50
Four honours in one hand	80
Five honours divided four-to-one	90
Four Aces in one hand	100
Five honours in one hand	100

● If a partnership bids and fulfils a doubled contract, the declarer scores 50 above the line and 50 for every overtrick.
● If a redoubled contact is bid and made, declarer's partnership earns 100 bonus points and 100 points for each overtrick.
● Declarer's opponents receive points above the line for each of the declarer's partnerships' undertricks as follows:

Undoubled contract	50 points
Doubled contract	100 points
Redoubled contract	200 points

Winning
● 30 points below the line wins a game and a line is drawn, as in Contract bridge.
● The first partnership to win two games wins that rubber and earns 250 extra points.

▶ A 19th-century English Queen of hearts

Euchre

Euchre is thought to have evolved from a Franco-German game known as Jucker. Introduced to the United States in the early 1800s, it quickly became popular among seamen. The Joker was invented for Euchre, to serve as top trump.

Objective

Partnerships attempt to win at least three out of five tricks.

Card values

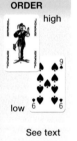

RANKING ORDER

high

low

See text

- The twenty-five card deck used in Euchre consists of Ace, King, Queen, Jack, 10 and 9 of each suit, plus one Joker. A two may be used instead of a Joker.
- The trump suit (see Deciding trumps, opposite) has eight cards. The Joker is the highest-ranking (no matter what the trump suit) followed by the Jack of the trump suit, the Jack of the suit that is the same colour as the trump suit (black or red), then Ace, King, Queen, ten and nine.

▶ Card ranking in a trump suit

- For the purposes of play, once the trump suit has been decided, the Joker and the Jack of the same-colour suit are effectively part of that suit and cannot be played as part of any other suit. For example, if the trump suit is clubs, the Jack of spades is played as if it were a second Jack of clubs and never as a Jack of spades.

Partnerships and dealing

- Partnerships are decided either randomly or by mutual consent. The first dealer is also selected at random and the dealership subsequently passes clockwise around the table.
- The dealer shuffles the cards, and the player to his left may elect to cut the cards before they are dealt.

- Players are dealt five cards each in two packets. The first packet consisting of three cards and the second of two.
- Once all four players have five cards, the dealer turns the next card face-up. This card, known as the 'upcard' is used in determining trumps. The remaining four cards are left face-down and play no further part in the hand. No player may look at his hand until the upcard is revealed.

Deciding trumps

- Once the upcard has been revealed, the player to the dealer's left has the option of accepting or rejecting the suit of that card as trumps.
- To accept the suit he calls 'I order it up'; to reject he calls 'I pass'.
- Passing clockwise around the table, the other two players in turn have an opportunity to accept or reject the suit of the upcard using the same calls.
- As soon as a player accepts the suit of the upcard, it becomes trumps and trick-taking play begins.
- The dealer may accept the suit of the upcard by discarding one card from his hand and replacing it with the upcard.
- If no players accept the upcard, a second round takes place in which the players, starting with the first to the dealer's left, may nominate any suit other than the suit of the upcard, or pass.
- As soon as a player nominates a suit, it becomes trumps and trick-taking play begins.
- If no player nominates a trump suit in the second round the hand is abandoned and a new dealer takes over.
- If the upcard is the Joker, the dealer must nominate a trump suit without first looking at his hand, then add the Joker to his hand and discard any other card.

Makers and defenders

- During trick-taking play the two partnerships are designated 'makers' or 'defenders'.
- A player who accepts the upcard or nominates a trump suit effectively nominates his partnership as makers and his opponents as defenders.
- A player who decides the trump suit may elect to play solo by calling 'I play alone'. His partner places his hand face-down on the table and plays no further part in the hand.
- Essentially, makers must attempt to win at least three of the five tricks in the trick-taking phase or suffer a points penalty. Defenders attempt to stop them from reaching this goal.

Playing

● If all four players are active in the hand, trick play is opened by the player to the dealer's left and passes in a clockwise direction.

● If a maker is playing solo, trick play is opened by the player to his left and passes in a clockwise direction.

● The opener may play any card from his hand face-up onto the table.

● The next player must follow the suit of the opener's card if he is able or, if he is not able, play a trump card or a card of any other suit.

● The trick is won by the highest-ranking card of the opening suit, or by the highest-ranking trump.

● The winner of a trick leads the next.

EXAMPLES OF PLAY

Example 1 of possible trick play:
1 All four players are active and hearts are trumps. The player to the dealer's left (player A) opens with 10♠. Spades are the lead suit.
2 The next player (B) follows suit with A♠.
3 Player C also follows suit with J♠.
4 The dealer (player D) also follows suit with K♠.
5 Player B wins the trick because he played the highest-ranking card of the lead suit and no trumps were played.

Example 2 of possible trick play:
1 All four players are active and hearts are trumps. The player to the dealer's left (player A) opens with Q♠. Spades are the lead suit.
2 Player B has no cards of the lead suit. He plays J♦. This is a trump card because it is the Jack of the suit of the same colour (red) as the trump suit (hearts).
3 Player C follows the lead suit with K♠.
4 Player D (the dealer) has no cards of the lead suit. He plays J♥.
5 Player D wins the trick because his trump, J♥, outranks player B's trump, J♦, and both outrank the lead suit.

Scoring

● At the end of a hand, scores are calculated according to the scoring table (see opposite page).

● The makers' goal of winning three out of five tricks, and the defenders' goal of preventing this, are reflected in the scoring system.

● A game is normally played to eleven points. With the first team to accumulate eleven or more points winning the game.

SCORING TABLE

No solo maker

Hand result	Makers	Defenders
3 or 4 tricks	1	0
5 tricks (a march)	2	0
Fewer than 3 tricks (euchre)	0	2

Solo maker

Hand result	Maker	Defenders
3 or 4 tricks	1	0
5 tricks (a march)	4	0
Fewer than 3 tricks (euchre)	0	4

● Makers that fail to win at least three of the five tricks in a hand are said to be 'euchred'.

● Traditionally, Euchre players use the two unused fives and the two sixes from the deck to record scores. The cards are arranged so that the number of pips showing represents a partnership's score.

◄ Using cards to show scores of 3, 4, 5 and 6 points

Strategy tips

● There are only twenty-five cards in a game of Euchre. Eight of these in any hand are in the trump suit. Given these proportions, it is reasonable to make educated guesses about the distribution of trumps around the table.

● On average, there is likely to be one trump in the four cards discarded after the deal and the player who calls trumps is likely to have at least two and probably three. That leaves four other trumps distributed among the other three players.

● Bearing these averages in mind can be very useful in the long term, although they cannot guarantee success in any single hand.

EUCHRE

151

MUST KNOW

Terminology

Euchre players often refer to the top three ranking cards by specific names:

Joker – Best Bower (or Bauer)

Jack of the trump suit – Right Bower (or Bauer)

Jack of the same colour as the trump suit – Left Bower (or Bauer)

Euchre variants

▶ **CALL-ACE EUCHRE**

- A variant for four to six players.
- All players are solo, except in the situation where the maker chooses to play with a partner.
- The maker chooses a partner by declaring 'I call on the Ace of (suit)', but the player who holds that Ace does not make his identity known until he plays the card.
- If the Ace has not been dealt, the maker effectively plays solo.
- Scoring differs as follows:

Hand result	Maker	Defender
3 or 4 tricks	1	0
5 tricks (a march)	1 per other player	0
Less than 3 tricks	0	2 per other player

▶ **NORTH AMERICAN EUCHRE**

- No Joker is used (no Best Bower), so there are only 24 cards in play.
- Otherwise, the rules are the same.

▶ **32-CARD EUCHRE**

- The 8s and 7s are included to make a playing deck of 32 cards. Sometimes the Joker is also used as Best Bower to make a deck of 33.
- 8s and 7s rank, as would be expected, below 9s.
- Otherwise, the rules are the same.

▶ A very early card from the 15th century depicting Sir Lancelot

Knaves

Knaves is a good place to start for players who are unfamiliar with trick-taking games before moving on to more developed forms of the genre such as Whist or Contract bridge. The rules are simple but playing successfully calls for careful thought and a considered strategy. A 'Knave' is another term for a Jack.

Objective
To win the most tricks while avoiding collecting Jacks (Knaves).

Card values
Knaves is played with a standard deck of 52 cards. The cards rank in their suits with Aces highest, followed by Kings, Queens, Jacks, tens, nines, eights, sevens, sixes, fives, fours, threes and twos (lowest).

Dealing
● The first dealer is chosen at random and the dealership subsequently passes in a clockwise direction.
● Twelve cards are dealt face-down and one at a time to each player. A thirteenth card is then dealt to each player other than the dealer.
● The last card is turned face-up on the table. The suit of this card becomes the trump suit for the deal. The dealer adds this card to his hand at the start of his first turn.

Playing
● Play begins with the first player to the dealer's left and proceeds in a clockwise direction.
● The first player may play any card face-up on the table. The suit of this card becomes the 'lead' suit for the trick.
● All players must follow the lead suit if they are able. If they do not have any cards of the lead suit, they may play a card of the trump suit or any other card in their hand.
● The highest-ranking card of the lead suit wins the trick unless a trump card has been played, in which case the highest-ranking trump wins. The winner of a trick leads (is the first to play) the next trick.
● Since each player has thirteen cards and plays one in each trick, there are thirteen tricks in a deal.

EXAMPLES OF PLAY

Example 1 of possible trick play:

1 Hearts are the trump suit. The player to the dealer's left (player A) opens with 8♠. Spades are the lead suit.
2 The next player (player B) follows suit with A♠.
3 Player C also follows suit with J♠.
4 The dealer (player D) also follows suit with K♠.
5 Player B wins the trick because he played the highest-ranking card of the lead suit (A♠) and no trumps were played.

Example 2 of possible trick play:

1 Hearts are the trump suit. Player A opens with Q♣. Clubs are the lead suit.
2 Player B has no cards of the lead suit. He plays a trump card, J♥.
3 Player C follows the lead suit with K♣.
4 Player D (the dealer) has no cards of the lead suit and also has no trump card that ranks higher than player B's J♥. He plays 4♦.
5 Player B wins the trick because his trump (J♥) outranks both cards of the lead suit.

Scoring

● At the end of each deal (thirteen tricks) players score one point for every trick they have taken.

● Points are subtracted from this total for any Jacks (or Knaves) a player has collected as part of any tricks he has won. These penalties are shown in the Scoring table below:

SCORING TABLE

Knave	Penalty points
Jack of hearts	-4
Jack of diamonds	-3
Jack of clubs	-2
Jack of spades	-1

● Play continues until a player wins by reaching 20 points or more.

● Penalties may also be applied to players who fail to follow the lead suit of a trick when they have a card of that suit in their hand. This is known as a 'revoke' and attracts a three-point penalty. Alternatively, three bonus points may be awarded to all other players when one player revokes.

Knaves variants

▶ POLIGNAC

- Polignac is a French variant of Knaves in which the Jack of spades is known as Polignac.
- As with Knaves, the objective of Polignac is to take as many tricks as possible while avoiding collecting Jacks.
- Rules are the same, except for the following variations:

Dealing

- Polignac is played with a deck of 32 cards – a standard 52-card deck is stripped of all 2s, 3s, 4s, 5s and 6s. Cards rank from Ace (highest) to 7 (lowest).
- Players receive eight cards each.
- There is no trump suit.

Playing

- Trick-taking is the same as in Knaves, except that there is no trump suit so the highest-ranking card of the lead suit wins.
- A player may declare, after the deal but before play begins, that he believes he can take all the tricks in a deal. This is known as playing 'general' and has its own point rewards and penalties.
- Before play starts, a maximum number of deals is decided and the game ends when that maximum has been reached.

Scoring

- Players receive one point for each trick taken and deduct points for each Jack collected as part of those tricks. The Jacks of hearts, diamonds and clubs carry one penalty point each. The Jack of spades (Polignac) carries two penalty points.

-2 points   -1 point each

- Completing a general play wins five bonus points. Failing a general play gives five points each to the other three players.
- The winner is the player with the most points after the agreed number of deals have been played.

Whist

NUMBER
OF CARDS

52

One deck
of 52 cards

RANKING
ORDER

high

A♠ A♠

A♥ A♥ ♠2

low ♣2 ♥ ♣2

Whist is the classic trick-taking game that forms the basis of Contract bridge. The earliest mention of Whist comes from English literature of the sixteenth century, and the earliest book devoted to the game was published in England in 1742. The word 'whist' is thought to derive from an Old English word meaning 'be silent', an appropriate name for a game in which communication is discouraged. Whist reached the United States in the 1890s, where it soon evolved into the more complex modern game of Bridge. Whist is a challenging, tactical game that is still widely played.

Objective

Partnerships attempt to win more than six tricks in each deal in order to accumulate points.

Card values

Whist is played with a standard deck of 52 cards. The cards rank in their suits with Aces highest, followed by Kings, Queens, Jacks, tens, nines, eights, sevens, sixes, fives, fours, threes and twos (lowest).

Partnerships and dealing

● Partnerships are chosen at random or by mutual consent and remain fixed throughout the game. Partners sit opposite each other.

● The first dealer is chosen at random and the dealership subsequently passes in a clockwise direction.

● Twelve cards are dealt face-down and one at a time to each player. A thirteenth card is then dealt to each player other than the dealer. The last card is turned face-up on the table. The suit of this card becomes the trump suit for the deal. The dealer adds this card to his hand at the start of his first turn.

● Traditionally, two decks of cards are used in a game of Whist. The second deck is shuffled by the dealer's partner during the deal so that it is ready for use in the next hand. It is not necessary to use two decks of cards.

● A misdeal may be declared if any player receives less than thirteen cards, or if any card other than the dealer's final card is revealed. In the case of a misdeal, the cards are reshuffled and passed to the next dealer.

Playing

● Play to the first trick begins with the first player to the dealer's left and proceeds in a clockwise direction around the table. The first player is said to 'lead' the trick.

● The first player may play any card face-up on the table. The suit of this card becomes the 'lead' suit for the trick. All players must follow the lead suit if they are able. If they do not have any cards of the lead suit, they may play a card of the trump suit or any other card in their hand.

● The trick is won by the player who contributes the highest-ranking card of the lead suit. If any trump cards are played, then the trick is won by the highest-ranking trump card. The winner of a trick leads the next trick. Since each player has thirteen cards and plays one in each trick, there are thirteen tricks in a deal.

EXAMPLES OF PLAY

Example 1 of possible trick play:

1 Hearts are the trump suit. The player to the dealer's left (player A) opens with A♣ (suppose this is the first trick). Clubs are the lead suit.

2 The next player (B) follows suit with 10♣.

3 Player C also follows suit with 6♣.

4 The dealer (player D) also follows suit with 2♣.

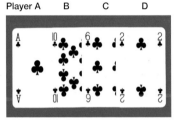

5 Player A wins the trick because he played the highest-ranking card of the lead suit and no trumps were played.

Example 2 of possible trick play:

1 Diamonds are the trump suit. Player A opens with 10♥. He leads the trick because he was the winner of the previous trick. Clubs are the lead suit.

2 Player B has no cards of the lead suit. He plays a trump card, 2♦.

3 Player C follows the lead suit with 8♥.

4 Player D (the dealer) follows the lead suit with 5♥.

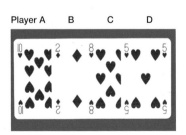

5 Player B wins the trick because his trump, 2♦, outranks all three cards of the lead suit.

- Play continues until all thirteen tricks in a deal have been played, at which point a new deal is made by the next dealer.
- A partnership that wins all thirteen tricks in a deal is said to have achieved a 'slam'.

Scoring

- No score is awarded for the first six tricks won in a deal. Each trick won in excess of the sixth earns one point. This means that, in a deal of thirteen tricks, it is possible for only one point to be won: one partnership wins six tricks, scoring nothing, and the other wins seven tricks, scoring one.
- Additional points may be won during a hand by partnerships holding 'honour' cards. The honour cards are the Ace, King, Queen and Jack of the trump suit for that hand. Four points are awarded to a partnership holding all four honour cards at the end of a deal; two points are awarded for holding three.
- Points won for tricks take precedence over points won for honour cards in the case of both partnerships reaching a total of five points in a deal.
- Five points win a game. Game-winning partners receive three extra points if their opponents have no score, two extra points if their opponents have one or two points, and one extra point if their opponents have a score of three or four.
- Seven points are needed to win a game under the rules usually played in the United States. This makes it more difficult for a partnership to win a game in a single deal.
- A rubber consists of three games. The first partnership to win two games wins the rubber. If a partnership wins the first two games of a rubber, the third is not played and that partnership receives two extra bonus points.
- The partnership with the most points at the end of a rubber wins the game.
- Penalty points can also be subtracted from players who 'revoke'. Revoking is failing to play a card of the lead suit when a player has one available in his hand. Usually, three points are lost by a partnership that revokes. Alternatively, three points may be awarded to their opponents or three points may be transferred from the revokers to their opponents. The form of penalty to be used, if any, should be mutually agreed before the game begins.
- A deal is usually played to the end, even when one partnership accumulates five or more points during play.

Whist variants

▶ **SOLO WHIST**
- Solo whist is a variant of Whist that includes a bidding phase.
- Bidding is a process during which players predict the number of tricks they will win, or fail to win. Accurate predictions bring points.
- The rules for Solo whist are essentially the same as for Whist except for the addition of rules for bidding and a different scoring system.

Bidding
- Bidding takes place once all the cards have been dealt and the last card has been turned face-up to indicate a possible trump suit. Starting with the player to the dealer's left, players may make the following bids:

Proposal and acceptance (or prop and cop)
A player undertakes to win eight tricks in temporary partnership with another player with the suit of the face-up card as trumps. This bid only comes into effect if a subsequent player accepts the proposal and becomes the original bidder's temporary partner.

Solo
A player undertakes to win five tricks playing alone against the other three and with the trump suit indicated by the last card of the deal.

Misère (or nullo)
A player undertakes to lose all tricks with no trump suit in play.

Abondance
A player undertakes to win nine tricks with a trump suit of his own choosing. The trump suit is not announced until bidding ends.

Royal abondance (or abondance in trumps)
A player undertakes to win nine tricks with the trump suit indicated by the last card of the deal.

Misère ouvert (or spread)
A player undertakes to lose all tricks with no trump suit in play and playing with his cards turned face-up.

Abondance declarée
A player undertakes to win all thirteen tricks with no trump suit in play.

- The bids are presented here in rank order, with the first having the lowest rank and the last the highest rank.
- The player who makes the highest-ranking bid is said to have won the bidding and is then required to fulfil that undertaking.
- Bids are cancelled by subsequent bids of a higher rank.

Whist variants continued...

- A player may make a second bid if his first bid has been outranked, or if he has made a proposal bid that has not been accepted.
- A player may choose to pass rather than make a bid. The bidding phase ends when three players in a row pass.
- Play begins with the player to the dealer's left, unless a bid of abondance declarée has been made, in which case the bidder leads.

Scoring
- There are specific point rewards and point penalties for successfully fulfilling each bid and for failing to fulfil each bid.

Proposal and acceptance
- One partner receives five points from one opponent, and the other partner receives five points from the other opponent.
- One point each is also transferred for every trick more than five won (overtricks).
- One point from each of the partners goes to the opponents for every trick short of the bid (undertricks).

▼ Cards from an early 19th-century deck depicting great French kings, their queens and sons

Other bids	Points
Solo wins	10 points
Misère wins	15 points
Abondance wins	20 points
Royal abondance wins	25 points
Misère ouverte wins	30 points
Abondance declarée wins	40 points

● For bids other than misère, misère ouverte and abondance declarée one extra point is awarded to the declarers for each overtrick, and one to their opponents for each undertrick.

▶ **ROTATING TRUMPS**
● In Whist tournaments the trump for each deal is often pre-determined rather than being determined by the last card dealt.
● In this case, the first deal is played with hearts as trumps, the second with diamonds as trumps, the third with spades and the fourth with clubs. The sequence then repeats.

games

for four +

Most card games for more than four players are gambling games, although they can be enjoyed without involving money. They tend to be fast-paced affairs in which the turn of one card can spell good fortune or instant disaster.

Blackjack

Blackjack is the world's most popular betting card game. It probably evolved from the French games Chemin de fer and French ferme and was first played in France at the beginning of the eighteenth century, when it was known as Vingt-et-un. Blackjack has been played in the United States since about 1800 and, most famously, in the casinos of Nevada since 1931. The same game is also known today as Pontoon and Twenty-one. The version of the game given here is slightly different from the casino version and is best suited to social play.

Objective

Players attempt to assemble a hand with a higher value than the dealer's hand without exceeding a value of twenty-one.

Card values

● Blackjack is played with a standard deck of 52 cards. Sometimes, two standard decks are shuffled together to make a deck of 104 cards. A Joker is sometimes also used as a marker.

● Cards have values as shown in the table below:

CARD VALUES

Card (any suit)	Value
Ace	10 or 1
King	10
Queen	10
Jack	10
Ten	10
Nine – two	Index value (9 – 2)

Dealing and betting

● In Blackjack, the dealer is also the bank. This means that he pays or receives payments according to bets made. The first dealer is chosen at random or by mutual consent. Subsequently, the dealership is passed around the table in a clockwise direction after each dealer has dealt five games. Alternatively the dealership may pass to a new player only after a game in which a 'natural' hand has been dealt. A natural hand is a hand in which the first two cards dealt have a combined value of exactly twenty-one. At the end of that game, the player who was dealt the natural has the opportunity to become the next dealer. If he refuses, the existing dealer has the opportunity to continue dealing. If the existing dealer also refuses, the dealership is offered to each player in turn, starting with the player to the dealer's left and continuing in a clockwise direction. If no player accepts the dealership, a new dealer is chosen in the same manner as the first dealer of the session. If two or more players are dealt naturals in a game, the player closest to the dealer's left has the first opportunity to accept or refuse the dealership, followed in the same clockwise order by any other players who were dealt naturals.

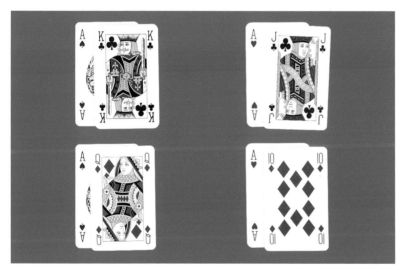

◄ Examples of natural hands

● Any player may shuffle the cards on his request. The dealer should always shuffle the cards before any deal and has the right to shuffle the cards after any other player has done so. After the dealer has shuffled, any other player should cut the cards. The Joker is then placed face-up at the bottom of the pack.

● The dealer decides and announces the maximum and minimum bets for the duration of his deal. Alternatively, a maximum and minimum may be set for the duration of the entire session by the mutual consent of all players before play begins.

● One card is dealt, face-down to each player, starting with the player on the dealer's left and moving in a clockwise direction. Each player then looks at his face-down card. All players, except the dealer, then place their bets on the table in front of them. The dealer may call for all bets to be doubled. Any player who refuses to double, loses his bet to the dealer. If a dealer has called for bets to be doubled, any player may then redouble his own bet, but only if his second card has not yet been dealt.

● A second card is dealt, face-up, to each player in the same order as the first cards were dealt. If the dealer has a natural hand, he immediately turns both of his cards face-up and collects double the amount bet by each player. Any other players who also have naturals only have to pay the dealer the amount of their bet. The cards are then collected for the next deal.

Playing

● If the dealer does not receive a natural, play begins with the player to the dealer's left. If that player has a natural, he immediately turns both his cards face-up and is paid by the dealer. If he does not have a natural, he may ask for another card, by calling 'I draw' or 'hit me' and the dealer will give him one more card, face-up. The player may ask for as many cards in succession as he wants. When the player is satisfied with the total count of the cards in his hand he calls 'I stand' or 'I stay'. If the total count of the player's cards exceeds twenty-one he must immediately declare the fact by calling 'I bust' and turn his cards face-up. The dealer then collects his bet and places the cards from his hand face-up at the bottom of the deck. A soon as a player calls 'I stand' or 'I bust', play passes to the next player to the left.

● All subsequent players proceed in the same manner as the first player to the dealer's left until only the dealer's hand is left to play.

● If all players have bust by the time the dealer's turn arrives, he discards his cards and a new deal is made. If at least one player remains in the game, the dealer turns his cards face-up and has the opportunity to draw further cards. He may call 'I draw' and deal himself as many face-up cards as he wants, or he may call 'I stand' and deal no more cards. If the dealer's total count exceeds 21, he calls 'I bust' and pays any players who are still in the game.

Doubling down

After looking at his first two cards, and when his turn comes around, a player may decide to 'double down'. To double down, he turns both his cards face-up, doubles his bet, and is dealt one more card, face-down, which he may not look at until the dealer's hand has been played.

Buying

After looking at his first two cards, and when his turn comes around, a player may decide to 'buy' a card. To buy a card, he must double his bet (he may more than double his bet if he wishes), and receives another card, dealt face-down, which he may inspect. A player may continue to buy as many cards as he wishes, or he may receive subsequent cards in the normal way. He must still declare if he is bust after buying a card.

Splitting pairs

● If the first two cards dealt to a player are a pair of the same rank, regardless of suit, the player may 'split' his hand when his turn comes around. To split his hand, a player turns both his cards face-up and separates them. His original bet is placed by one card, and a new bet of at least the same amount is placed by the other. The dealer than deals one card face-up next to one of the player's original cards. The player may then stand, draw, buy or double down in the same way as for a normal hand. He then receives another card, face-up next to his other original card and plays another hand in the normal way.

● If the card dealt to either, or both, of the original cards makes another pair, the player may split that pair also. This applies to all subsequent pairs created in the same way. If the original pair were Aces, and the player splits them, he is not paid for a natural. If the first card dealt to either of the split pair gives a total count of twenty-one, the player is also not paid for a natural.

Settling

● If the dealer goes bust, he pays all players who have not gone bust. If the dealer does not go bust, he pays all players who stood at totals greater than his own and collects the bets of all players who stood at totals less than his own. If a player's total is the same as the dealer, the dealer collects the bet. Alternatively, the bet may be returned to the player.

● The dealer pays players by giving them the same amount as their bet, unless the player has a natural, in which case he gives that player twice the amount of his bet.

● As each bet is settled, that player's cards are collected by the dealer and placed face-up at the bottom of the deck. Play continues from the remainder of the deck until the Joker is uncovered. All the cards below the Joker (cards that have previously been played) are then shuffled and cut in the normal way, and the Joker is again placed face-up at the bottom. Play continues using the newly-shuffled cards.

EXAMPLE OF PLAY

Example of play with four players plus the dealer:

▶ Example of play in progress

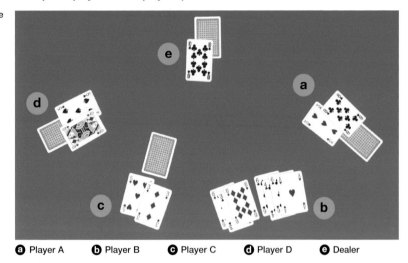

ⓐ Player A   **ⓑ** Player B   **ⓒ** Player C   **ⓓ** Player D   **ⓔ** Dealer

1   The dealer's first card was an 8 and his second card is a 10. He does not have a natural, so play continues.

2   Player A's first card was a Jack and his second card was a 3. He does not have a natural and decides to draw another card, which is an 8. He now has a total of twenty-one and stands.

3   Player B's first card was a 6 and his second card was also a 6. He does not have a natural and decides to split his pair of sixes. The first card dealt to his 6♦ is a 3. He draws another card and receives a 10. He stands on that hand with a total of nineteen. The first card dealt to his 6♠ is a four. He draws another card and receives a 6. He draws another card and receives an Ace. Because Aces can be counted as one or eleven, he is not bust and stands with a total of seventeen.

4   Player C's first card was a 3 and his second card was a 5. He does not have a natural. He decides to double down and receives a Queen (although he does not know what he has received at this point).

5   Player D's first card was a 7 and his second card was a 5. He does not have a natural. He decides to draw another card and receives a Queen. Player B is bust because his total has exceeded twenty-one (7 + 5 + 10 (Queen) = 22). The dealer collects his bet.

6   The dealer has a total of eighteen and decides to stand. Player C's Queen is revealed, giving him a total of eighteen. The dealer must pay player A and player B for one of his hands (the one with a total of nineteen). He collects the bet for player B's other hand, and for player C's hand.

Bonuses

- Certain hands force the dealer to pay out on a player's bet no matter what the dealer's final total is. If a player has a hand with five cards and has not gone bust, the dealer immediately pays him double the bet. If a player has a hand with six cards without going bust, the dealer immediately pays him four times the bet. For a hand of eight cards the pay-out is eight times the bet, and so on.

- If a player makes a total of twenty-one with three 7s, he is paid three times his bet. If a player makes a total of twenty-one with an 8, a 7 and a 6, he is paid twice his bet.

- None of these hands have any consequences if held by the dealer.

Strategy tips

- The most important strategic decision to be made in Blackjack is deciding when to stand and when to draw. There are two situations in which the decision is simple. If your cards have a total of nine or less, you should draw at least one more card, because it would be impossible for you to go bust no matter what that card was. If your cards have a total of seventeen or more, you should stand, because the chances of another card sending you bust are very high.

- The only way to make a rational decision about what to do when your hand has a total of more than nine but less than seventeen is to count cards. Card counting in Blackjack is often considered to be a form of cheating, especially by casinos. In fact, it is the same strategy that any rational player would adopt in almost any card game. Card counting essentially means watching and remembering which cards have already been played so that you know which cards remain in the deck. The reason that card counting has a bad reputation in casinos is because many cheats have resorted to the use of concealed electronic devices to help them calculate the odds. Casino Blackjack is routinely played with a deck made up of six or eight standard decks, making the odds and numbers that a card counter has to retain in his head extremely complex. Theoretically, keeping a perfect count of cards played in a casino game should enable a player to beat the dealer more times than he is beaten in the long term. Unfortunately, the 'long term' probably amounts to several million hands. In a social game, with only 52 cards in the deck, you might have a chance of keeping track of the number of cards with a value of ten that have been played.

- It is almost always a good idea to split pairs when they are eights or below, so you have two hands that can safely be drawn on.

Blackjack variants

▶ US BLACKJACK

● There are many slightly different forms of Blackjack played throughout the world. Many casinos have their own versions. The most radical variation is the different method of dealing and betting that is common to many US versions of the game. In casino games, the dealership always remains with the casino's own dealer.

Dealing and betting

● Players make their bets before any cards are dealt. The dealer deals one card, face-down, to each player and then one card, face-up, to himself. A second card is then dealt, face-down, to each player including the dealer.

● If the dealer's face-up card is an Ace or has a value of ten, he immediately looks at his face-down, or 'hole' card, to see if he has a natural. If the dealer has a natural, he turns both cards face-up and announces the natural. All the other players turn their cards face-up and the dealer collects the bets of those players who do not also have naturals. A player who has a natural in this situation has his bet returned.

● If the dealer's face-up card is not an Ace and does not have a value of ten, or if it is but the dealer does not have a natural, play begins with the first player to the dealer's left.

Playing

● Doubling down is more frequently allowed than card buying if the rules for dealing and betting given above are being used. Sometimes, doubling down is only allowed if a player's first two cards have a combined total of ten or eleven. Splitting pairs is almost always allowed.

Settling and bonuses

● The rules for settling and bonuses are the same.

▶ IRREGULAR DEALS

● The most important rules that concern irregularities are:
1) A player who is dealt two initial cards may discard either one or play with two hands.
2) A player who is dealt two second cards may discard either one.
3) A player who stands on a total of more than twenty-one pays twice his bet.

Brag

Brag is a British game and one of the ancestors of modern Poker. The game was certainly well known in England in the late eighteenth century and was probably played long before then. The form described here is known as Three-card brag. It is the oldest and still the most popular version today.

Objective
Players try to win a 'pot' or 'pool' by having the highest-ranking hand or by being the last player to drop out of the betting.

Card values
● Brag is played with a standard deck of 52 cards. Cards in their suits rank with the Ace highest, followed by King, Queen, Jack, ten, nine, eight, seven, six, five, four, three and two (lowest).
● The Ace may also rank as the lowest card for the purposes of making sequences.

NUMBER OF CARDS

52

One deck of 52 cards

RANKING ORDER

high

low

See text

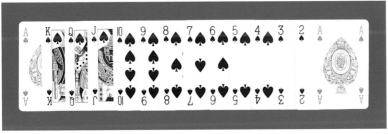

High   Low

◄ Card ranking

Preparing
● Before play begins, players must agree on:
   a) The 'ante': the amount that every player must contribute to the pot before each deal (this may be nothing).
   b) The minimum and maximum initial bet: the amount that the first player must place in the pot in order to stay in the deal (for example, a minimum of two chips and a maximum of five).
   c) The betting limit: the maximum amount that the bet can be increased by subsequent players (for example, six chips).
● All players must be aware of any rule variations that are to be used in the session, such as the use of wild cards (see Brag variants, page 177).

Dealing and betting

- The first dealer is chosen at random, or by mutual consent, and the dealership subsequently passes in a clockwise direction.

- Before the first deal is made, the cards are shuffled by the dealer. Cards are not normally shuffled before subsequent deals in the session. Before each deal, every player must place his ante in the pot, unless an ante of zero has been agreed before the session starts.

- Each player, including the dealer, receives three cards, dealt face-down and one at a time. Players may look at their cards immediately, or may choose to play 'blind', in which case they may not examine their cards until later in the deal.

- Betting begins with the player on the dealer's left and proceeds in a clockwise direction.

- The first player may 'fold' or make a bet of any amount between the agreed minimum and maximum. A player who folds discards his hand and takes no further part in the deal. His cards must remain face-down on the table.

- If the first player folds, the next player has the same options as the first player had. If all the players fold, the last player automatically collects the contents of the pot.

- If the first player bets, the next player may fold or make a bet that is equal to or greater than the first player's bet. Each subsequent player has the option of folding or making a bet that is equal to or greater than the last bet made.

- Betting continues around the table until there are only two players who have not folded. At this point, the next player has the additional option of 'seeing' his opponent's hand. To see an opponent's hand, a player must place twice the last bet made in the pot. The opponent must then turn his cards face-up on the table. If the opponent's hand is of an equal or higher ranking than the hand belonging to the player who paid to see it, the opponent wins the pot and the player who paid does not expose his cards. If the opponent's hand is of a lower ranking, the player who paid to see it exposes his cards and wins the pot. Hands are ranked as shown in the table on the opposite page.

- Hands which do not contain any of the combinations shown in the table on the opposite page are ranked according to the individual cards they contain. The highest cards are compared first. If they are of equal rank, the next-highest cards are compared and if they too are of equal rank, the last cards are compared. When comparing by this method, and for all of the combinations shown opposite, it is possible for hands to be equal in rank.

Hand	Examples	
Prial	3♣ 3♦ 3♠ A♠ A♥ A♣ 2♦ 2♠ 2♥	'Prial' is an abbreviation of 'Pair royal'. A prial hand is a hand in which all three cards are the same rank. The highest-ranking prial is a hand of threes, next is a hand of Aces and then hands of Kings, Queens, Jacks, tens, nines, eights, sevens, sixes, fives, fours and twos (lowest).
Running flush	A♠ 2♠ 3♠ A♥ K♥ Q♥ 2♣ 3♣ 4♣	A sequence of three consecutively-ranked cards from the same suit, also known as an 'On a bike' run. Ace, two and three is the highest-ranking running flush; Ace, King and Queen is next; then King, Queen and Jack and so on down to two, three and four.
Run	A♠ 2♥ 3♣ A♥ K♣ Q♠ 2♥ 3♦ 4♣	A sequence of three consecutively-ranked cards from different suits. Ace, two and three is the highest-ranking run; Ace, King and Queen is next; then King, Queen and Jack and so on down to two, three and four.
Flush	A♥ K♥ J♥ 2♦ 3♦ 5♦	A set of three cards from the same suit that are not consecutive. Flushes are ranked against each other by comparing the highest card they contain first, to see which hand has the highest, then the middle card and finally the third card.
Pair	A♠ A♠ K♥ 2♦ 2♦ 3♠	A hand that contains two cards of the same rank in the same suit and a third card of a different rank. Pairs are ranked against each other by comparing the rank of the pair first, to see which hand has the highest and then the rank of the third card.

Hands are ranked in the order shown here, with prials the highest and pairs the lowest.

BRAG

● Betting continues until there is only one player who has not folded, or until one player pays to see his last remaining opponent's cards.

EXAMPLE OF PLAY

Example of betting in a game with five players:

Round	Player A	Player B	Player C	Player D	Player E
1	1	1	1	FOLD	2
2	2	2	2		4
3	4	FOLD	4		5
4	5		FOLD		10
5	10				10
6	20				
	(TO SEE)				

1 Player A opens with a bet of one chip. Players B and C decide to stay in the game and make the same bets. Player D folds and takes no further part in the deal. Player E raises the betting to two chips.

2 In order to stay in the game, players must bet at least two chips, since the last bet made was of two chips. Players A, B and C all bet two chips. Player E raises the bet again to four chips.

3 Players must now bet at least four chips to stay in the game. Player A bets four chips, player B folds and player C also bets four chips. Player E raises his bet again to five chips.

4 Players must now bet at least five chips to stay in the game. Player A bets five chips, but player C folds. Player E raises his bet again to ten chips.

5 Only players A and E remain in the game. Player A could pay 20 chips to see player E's cards, but instead he matches his bet of ten chips. Player E bets another ten chips. He too could have paid 20 chips to see player A's hand.

6 Player A pays 20 chips to see player E's hand. Betting ends.

Playing blind

● A player may choose to play blind once he has been dealt his cards (see Dealing and betting, page 172). A player who is playing blind takes part in the betting in the same way as other players, but his bets are regarded as doubled. This means that a player only has to bet a minimum of half the last bet made.

● A player playing blind may choose to look at his cards at any time, but after he has done so his bets cease to be regarded as double.

● If there are only two players left and one or both of them are playing blind, the option to see an opponent's hand is subject to special rules. A player who is not playing blind (an 'open' player) may not see the cards of a player who is playing blind. An open player's only options in this situation are to continue betting in the normal way or to fold. If both players are playing blind, either one may pay to see the other's cards by paying twice the minimum bet for a blind player. This would be the same as the minimum bet for an open player in the same situation. A blind player may pay to see an open opponent's cards by paying twice the minimum bet for a blind player.

EXAMPLE OF PLAY

Example of betting in a game with five players, two of whom are playing blind:

Round	Player A (OPEN)	Player B (BLIND)	Player C (OPEN)	Player D (BLIND)	Player E (OPEN)
1	2	1	2	1	2
2	2	1	4	2	FOLD
3	4	4	8	FOLD	
4	FOLD	4	8		
5		8 (TO SEE)			

1 Player A opens with a bet of two chips. Player B (playing blind) has to bet one chip to stay in the game (half of the bet required for an open player). Player C stays in the game by making the required two-chip bet. Player D (playing blind) also makes the minimum bet, as does player E.
2 Player A makes the minimum bet, as does player B. Player C increases his bet to four chips. The minimum bid for player D is now two chips, which he makes. Player E folds.
3 Player A makes the minimum bet of four chips. Player B raises his bet to four chips, open players must now bet eight chips to stay in the game. Player C makes the minimum bet of eight chips. Player D folds.
4 Player A folds. Player B now has the option of seeing player C's cards, but decides to make the minimum bet of four chips instead. Player C may not pay to see player B's cards because an open player may not pay to see a blind player's cards. Player C makes the minimum bet of eight chips.
5 Player B exercises his option to see his open opponent's cards by paying eight chips. Betting ends.

● If all the players fold apart from a blind player, the blind player retains his hand and a second hand is dealt to him in the usual way in the next deal. That player must then choose whether to examine the hand from the previous deal, examine the new hand or examine neither hand. He may not examine both hands. If the player chooses to look at one of the hands he may decide to keep that hand and discard the other, in which case he is no longer playing blind, or discard that hand and keep the other. If he discards the hand he has looked at he may continue playing blind with the other hand, or look at it and continue as an open player.

● If a player decides not to look at either hand, he plays the next deal with two blind hands. He may choose to look at either one of his hands during the course of the deal and revert to open play, or he may look at neither and continue to play blind. A player who wins a deal with two blind hands must discard one of them, unexamined, before the next deal.

● All folded cards are collected unexamined, and placed at the bottom of the deck before the next deal takes place. The winner's cards are also collected and placed at the bottom of the deck. If the winner's hand was blind, no player may examine the cards. If the winner's hand was open and was not seen, no player may examine the cards. In these cases, the cards are not shuffled before the next deal. If the winner's hand was seen or if the winner's hand was seen and his last opponent's hand was revealed, the cards are shuffled before the next deal.

MUST KNOW

Strategy tips

● Because there are no opportunities to change your hand there is nothing you can do to improve your chance of holding a winning hand. Because opponents' cards are rarely seen, and only ever at the end of the betting sequence, you have practically no information about what cards your opponents might be holding. Some authors maintain that Brag, like Poker, is not really a card game at all, but a betting game that happens to involve cards. It is certainly true that there are few strategic decisions that a Brag player has to make, and that they are all betting decisions.

● Betting decisions can be based on the probabilities of certain hands appearing in a deal. The approximate probabilities are shown below:

Hand	Probability
Prial of threes	1 in 5525
Any prial	1 in 460
Running flush	1 in 460
Run	1 in 31
Flush	1 in 20
Pair	1 in 6

● Players who bet or fold exclusively according to the odds are unlikely to win in the long-term against players who occasionally bluff.

▶ FOUR-CARD BRAG
- Four-card brag is a variant of Brag with a different dealing system.

Dealing and betting
- Players are dealt four cards each and must discard any one of them before betting begins. Discarded cards are kept face-down on the table by the player.
- Hands are ranked in the same way as in Brag, except that in the case of a tie between two hands, the discarded card is also examined and the player with the highest-ranking card wins.

Playing blind
- Players playing blind keep all four cards face-down. If a player looks at a blind hand and reverts to open play, he must discard a card.

▶ FIVE-CARD BRAG
- Five-card brag is a variant of Brag with a different dealing system.
- Players receive five cards each during the deal and discard two of them before betting begins.
- Both discards are used to settle tied hands.

▶ WILD CARDS
- Brag, as well as Four-card and Five-card brag, is sometimes played with wild cards. Wild cards are more commonly allowed in games of Four-card and Five-card brag.
- A wild card, is a card that can be used in place of any other card. If, for example, all twos were wild cards, a player could designate a two in his hand as standing for a card that would make his hand higher-ranking. A hand containing the cards A♠, A♠ and 2♥ has a high-ranking pair but if the two is a wild card it can be nominated as another Ace to make a high-ranking Prial.
- There are no fixed conventions about which cards are counted as wild cards, if any. The most common choices are: all the twos, the black twos (spades and clubs), all the Jacks, the black Jacks or one or more Joker added to the pack.
- Wild cards are usually taken to affect the ranking of hands. A hand with one or more wild card will always be beaten by a hand of the same rank with no wild cards. A hand with wild cards will only beat a hand of the same rank that contains more wild cards.

BRAG

177

Loo

**NUMBER
OF CARDS**

One deck
of 52 cards

Loo is an interesting game that is little known today but was notorious in Britain in the eighteenth and nineteenth centuries. Its notoriety was largely due to the opportunities it provided for players to bet and lose huge sums of money. Loo reached Britain from France, where it had long been played under the name Lenturlu, around 1660. The top trump in Loo is known as the 'Pam', an abbreviation of Pamphilus – a fictional medieval figure with loose morals whose name also gave us the word 'pamphlet'.

**RANKING
ORDER**

high

low

Objective

Players try to win at least one trick to avoid having to pay into the pool.

Card values

Loo is played with a standard deck of 52 cards. Cards in their suits rank with Ace highest, followed by King, Queen, Jack, ten, nine, eight, seven, six, five, four, three and two (lowest).

▶ Card
ranking

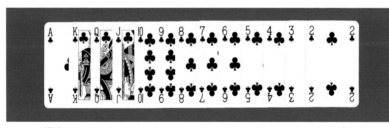

High   Low

Dealing

● The first dealer is chosen at random, or by mutual consent, and the dealership subsequently passes in a clockwise direction. The dealer must place three chips or counters in the pool and shuffle the cards before the deal is made. When the pool contains three chips it is known as a 'single'. If it contains more than three chips because there are chips remaining from previous deals, it is known as a 'double'.

● Three cards are dealt to each player, face-down and one at a time. Three cards are dealt in the same way to a spare hand known as the 'Miss'. The next card is turned face-up on the table and is known as the 'upcard'. The suit of the upcard is the trump suit for that deal.

Announcing

● The player on the dealer's left examines his cards and decides whether to play or not. If he decides not to play, he discards his hand face-down on the table. If he decides to play he may keep the cards he has or discard them in favour of the Miss hand but he may not examine the Miss hand first or go back to his original hand.

● If the first player did not take the Miss hand, the next player may choose to do so. Alternatively he may discard his hand or play with the hand he was dealt. Each player in turn has the same options, unless a player takes the Miss hand, in which case no subsequent player may exchange his cards.

● If all players discard their hands, the dealer wins the contents of the pool and a new deal is made by the next dealer. If one player takes the Miss hand and all the other players (including the dealer) pass, that player wins the pool. If only one player decides to play before the dealer's turn comes around, and he does not take the Miss hand, the dealer may not pass. He must play his own hand or take the Miss hand and play it. If he takes the Miss hand he may choose to play 'in defence of the Miss' which means that he does not win or lose anything for the play of that hand.

◄ Cards dealt for Loo with five players

a Player A's hand **b** Player B's hand **c** Player C's hand **d** Player D's hand
e Player E's hand **f** Miss hand **g** Upcard

Playing

● Play begins with the player to the dealer's left and passes in a clockwise direction. The first player must put his highest-ranking trump card face-down on the table. If he does not have a trump card, he must place the highest-ranking card he has in any other suit. The suit of the card that the first player plays is known as the 'lead' suit of the trick.

● The next player must play his highest trump card, if he has one. If he has no trump cards he must play the highest-ranking card he has in the lead suit (which may be the same as the trump suit). If he has no cards in the lead suit, he may play any other card from his hand. Play to the trick continues in this manner until all players have contributed one card.

● The trick is won by the highest-ranking card of the trump suit, or the highest-ranking card of the lead suit if no trumps were played. The winner of a trick leads the next trick. Three tricks are played in this manner.

EXAMPLES OF PLAY

Example of possible trick play with five players and clubs as trumps:

Trick	Player A	Player B	Player C	Player D	Player E
1	10♣ (LEAD)	8♣	K♣	J♦	A♠
2	7♥ (LEAD)	J♥	9♥	3♣	7♦
3	5♥ (LEAD)	8♠	Q♦	4♠	2♦

Trick 1 Clubs is the lead suit and the trump suit. Player C wins the trick because his King outranks any other trump card played.

Trick 2 Hearts is the lead suit. Player D wins the trick because his three was the only, and therefore the highest-ranking, trump card played.

Trick 3 Hearts is the lead suit. Player A wins the trick because his was the only, and therefore the highest-ranking, card played in the lead suit.

Note that, for the purposes of this example, player A leads each suit.

Settlement

● Each trick won by a player entitles that player to a one-third share of the pool. If the pool was a single at the start of the deal (contained only three chips), a player winning one trick would receive one chip, a player winning two tricks would receive two chips and a player winning all three chips would win the entire pool.

● A player who does not win any tricks is said to be 'looed' and is required to pay three chips into the pool after the winning players have taken their chips. These chips remain in the pool for the next deal.

Strategy tips

● Because of the rules that compel players to play their strongest cards first, there is nothing you can do to improve your chances of winning tricks once trick-play has started.

● The only strategic decisions to be made are whether or not to play with a hand at all and whether or not to exchange your hand for the Miss, if it is available.

● Hands that contain two trump cards will usually win at least one trick. Most hands will not contain any trumps and the majority of hands that do contain trumps will have only one. This means that all the trumps that have been dealt are almost always played to the first trick and that, therefore, any trump you play to the second trick is likely to win it. Hands that contain higher-ranking cards are obviously more useful than hands of low-ranking cards. Taking the Miss hand if you have a poor hand rather than discarding that hand is a pure gamble, but the Miss is unlikely to be worse.

Loo variants

▶ **FIVE-CARD LOO**

● Five-card loo is a variant of Loo with an additional trump card.

Card values

● The Jack of clubs is the top-ranking trump card and is known as the 'Pam'. The Pam is considered to be a part of whichever suit is trumps and ranks higher than any other card.

Dealing and betting

● Players receive five cards each and the dealer must contribute five chips to the pool. No Miss is dealt.

● A player who is dealt five cards from the same suit, or four cards from the same suit plus the Pam (known as a 'flush'), automatically wins everything in the pool. If two or more players have flushes, they are compared to see which contains the highest-ranking cards and the player with the highest-ranking flush wins the pool.

● A player may discard any number of cards from his hand and is dealt the same number of new cards by the dealer. Players may decide not to take part in the deal.

● A player who takes part in the deal undertakes to win at least one trick.

LOO

181

Rummy

NUMBER
OF CARDS

One deck
of 52 cards

Rummy is probably the second most commonly played card game in the English-speaking world. Early forms of Rummy evolved from a Mexican card game called Conquian and first appeared around the beginning of the twentieth century.

Objective

To dispose of all the cards in your hand before any other player.

RANKING
ORDER

high

low

Card values

Rummy is played with a standard deck of 52 cards. Cards in their suits rank with King highest, followed by Queen, Jack, ten, nine, eight, seven, six, five, four, three, two and Ace (lowest).

Dealing

- The first dealer is chosen at random or by mutual consent and the dealership subsequently passes in a clockwise direction.
- The number of cards dealt depends on the number of players. Two players receive ten cards each; three to four players, seven cards each; five or more players, six cards each. Cards are dealt face-down and one at a time, starting with the player on the dealer's left.
- Once the correct number of cards has been dealt to each player, the remainder of the pack is placed face-down in the centre of the table to form the stock. The top card from the stock pile is placed, face-up, next to it to start the discard pile.

Playing

- Play passes in a clockwise direction, starting with the player on the dealer's left.
- A player must draw a card from the top of either the discard pile or the stock pile and must, at the end of that turn, place a card from the hand face-up on the discard pile.
- After drawing a card from the stock or the discard pile a player may 'meld' or 'lay off'.

Melding

- A player may meld cards in the hand in two ways: in groups or in sequences of three or more cards.

Melding groups

● A group meld is a set of three or four cards of the same face value. For example J♥, J♦, J♠ or 7♥, 7♦, 7♠, 7♣ are both group melds.

● Group melds should be placed face-up in front of the player who made them.

Melding sequences

● A sequence meld is a set of three or four cards of the same suit with sequential face values. For example 4♦, 5♦, 6♦ or 9♣, 10♣, J♣, Q♣ are both sequence melds

● Sequence melds should be placed face-up in front of the player who made them.

▼ Example of a group meld and a sequence meld

| Group meld | Sequence meld |

Laying off

● 'Laying off' is placing an appropriate card in the hand alongside a meld that has previously been made by another player.

● A player may lay off one or more cards alongside existing group melds if the card or cards are of the same face value as the meld, or alongside existing sequence melds if the face value of the card or cards follows or precedes the sequence of the meld.

EXAMPLE OF PLAY

Example of possible play if the two melds shown above have been made and the player has the following cards:

6♥, 4♦, 3♦, 2♦, J♣, A♠, 3♣

1   Place the sequence meld 4♦, 3♦, 2♦ face-up on the table.
2   Lay off the 6♥ alongside the existing 6♣, 6♠, 6♦ meld.
3   Lay off the J♣ alongside the existing 8♣, 9♣, 10♣ meld.
4   Discard one other card.

Ending a turn

- Once a player has melded or laid off cards, if possible, one card from his hand must be discarded to finish his turn.
- A player may not discard a card that was picked up from the discard pile at the start of the same turn.
- To discard a card, a player places it face-up on the discard pile.
- If there are no more cards left in the stock pile, the discard pile is turned face-down to become the new stock pile and the top card is turned face-up to make a new discard pile.

Ending a hand

- Usually, a hand ends when one player has no more cards. This is known as 'going out'.
- A player's last card may be part of a meld, a lay off or it may be discarded. For example, a player with one card picks up another card from the stock at the beginning of a turn. If one of these cards can be laid off, the other can then be discarded and the player has won the hand. Alternatively, both cards may be laid off if that is possible and again, the player has won the hand.
- When all the cards in a player's hand are melded in the same turn, without that player having previously melded or laid off any cards, it is known as 'going rummy'.

Scoring

- When one player goes out, the value of the cards still held by all the other players is added up (see Card values table below).
- The player who won the hand receives points equal to the total value of the other players' cards.
- If the winning player went rummy, the points value is doubled.
- The first player to reach or exceed an agreed number of points wins the game.
- Games are commonly played to 301 or 501 points.

CARD VALUES

Card	Points
A – 10	Equal to face value
J, Q, K	10 points each
Rummy	All points doubled

Strategy tips

• Observation is the key to winning a game of Rummy.

• Try to keep track of which cards your opponents pick up from the discard pile. A player who picks up first one 6, then another is almost certainly trying to make a group meld of sixes.

• Also note which cards your opponents discard. If a player has been consistently picking up spades, and then discards a high-value spade, you can safely conclude that they are trying to make a low-value sequence meld of spades.

• You also need to be aware that any card you pick up or discard gives the same information to your opponents. It's sometimes worth picking up a card you don't need as a red herring.

• Be aware of the possibilities of completing melds. If you have two partial melds in your hand and need to discard, think about which meld is more likely to be completed first. For example, the hand 1♠, 2♠, 7♣, 8♣ has two partial sequences. The only way to complete a spade sequence is with the 3♠. A club sequence can be completed with either the 6♣ or the 9♣. Therefore, it would be more sensible to discard one of the spades than to discard one of the clubs.

• Don't forget to check everything already on the table for lay-off opportunities, not just your own melds.

Rummy variants

▶ **GIN RUMMY**

  • The rules of Gin rummy can be found in Games for two (see page 72).

▶ **ACES HIGH OR LOW**

  • Some players allow the Ace to be played as both high and low so that an Ace can be used in the sequence meld Ace, 2, 3 as well as the sequence meld Queen, King, Ace.

  • When playing by this rule, the Ace is given a point value of fifteen to reflect its increased usefulness.

▶ **LAST DISCARD**

  • In this variant, a player's last action before going out must be to discard a card. Players may not meld all their cards leaving nothing to discard.

Glossary of terms

bella In Kalabriasz, the King and Queen of the trump suit.

bezique A card game and a meld of the Queen of spades and the Jack of diamonds in that game.

book In Contract bridge, the first six tricks in a deal.

bower In Euchre, the Joker (best bower). In Five hundred, the Jack of the trump suit (right bower) and the Jack of the suit of the same colour as the trump suit (left bower).

brisque In Bezique, a trick containing a ten or an Ace which wins points for the player who captures it.

build In solitaire games, to place a card onto a card in the layout that immediately precedes or succeeds it in rank. The cards may have to be of the same suit or of a suit of the opposite or the same colour depending on the specific rules of the game. In Casino, to add a card to a card or cards in the layout so that the total value of the cards allows them to be captured on the next turn.

canasta The name of a card game for four players and a meld of seven cards of the same rank in that game.

capot In Piquet, winning all twelve tricks.

carte blanche A hand containing no court cards.

court cards The King, Queen and Jack of a suit.

▲ Eighteenth-century French court cards

crib In Cribbage, four cards (two from each player) that are discarded from the players' hands before play.

cut To divide the deck into two portions after the deal and to transpose their positions so that the cards that were formerly in the top part of the deck end up in the bottom part.

deal To distribute the required number of cards to each player. Also, the period of play between one deal and the next.

deck The complete set of cards used for a particular game.

declare To make a statement about your hand. Declarations should be made using only the terminology laid down in the rules of a game.

deuce A common term for the two of each suit.

declarer The player who makes the last bid in a trick-taking game.

discard To remove a card from your hand. Discarded cards are usually placed on a discard pile that other players may have access to, or kept face-down near the player.

dix In Kalabriasz, the seven of the trump suit. In Pinochle, the nine of the trump suit.

dummy In Contract bridge, the declarer's partner who does not play his hand. His cards are turned face-up and played by the declarer in the normal turn sequence.

elder hand The player to the dealer's left: usually the player who is the first to be dealt cards and the first to play. In two-player games, elder hand is the dealer's opponent.

face value The name of a card. For example King of diamonds (K ♦) or seven of hearts (7 ♥).

flush A hand in which all the cards are from the same suit. A flush often outranks other hands or melds.

follow suit To play a card of the same suit as the previously played card or of the same suit as the first card played to a trick.

forehand In Skat and others, the player to the dealer's left.

foundation In solitaire games, the card or cards on which the player attempts to build complete suits in order to win the game. Aces are common foundation cards.

going gin In Gin rummy, to lay all of your cards face-up on the table in valid melds.

going out In solitaire games, to rearrange all the cards in the layout into the desired final arrangement successfully. This usually means building all the cards, in sequence within their suits, onto the foundation cards. In Rummy, to meld all of your cards and discard the last one.

▲ A selection of modern Jokers

hand The cards dealt to a player to be used during play.

index value The number of pips on a card. The number in the corners of standard modern playing cards are known as the index numbers.

joker An extra card supplied with most modern decks of playing cards that is not part of any of the four suits. Jokers are commonly used as wild cards or as top-ranking trump cards. The Joker was invented by Euchre players to serve as the top trump.

kitty In games that are played for money (or counters), the pot of money (or counters) that players must contribute to in order to take part in a deal and in which they place any bets made. A player who wins the deal usually collects the contents of the kitty.

knave A common term for the Jack of each suit.

knock In Gin rummy, to lay valid melds face-up on the table. This is preceded by physically rapping on the table.

layout In solitaire games, the cards that are placed on the table before play begins. In Casino, an initial row of four face-up cards dealt to the table before play begins.

lead suit The suit of the first card played to a trick.

maker In many trick games, the player who decides the trump suit either by accepting the suit of an upcard or by proposing a suit.

matadors In Skat, the Jack of clubs plus any unbroken sequence of trumps after it in a hand.

meld A group of cards of the same suit or in numerical sequence. Also, to lay a group of cards on the table or to add appropriate cards to an existing meld.

middlehand In Skat and others, the second player to the dealer's left.

misdeal To deal the cards incorrectly.

no trump In Contract bridge and other games, when play takes place with no suit designated as trumps.

▲ A meld of
19th-century
German cards

overtrick In Contract bridge and other trick-taking games, tricks that are won by a player or a partnership in excess of their bid.

packet Two or more cards that are dealt to a player at the same time.

partie In Piquet, a complete game consisting of six deals.

pass A player's decision not to play or not to bid.

pinochle The name of a card game and a meld of the Queen of spades and the Jack of diamonds in that game.

pips The set of suit characters printed in the centre of standard modern playing cards. For example, the three diamonds printed in the centre of the three of diamonds.

piquet deck A playing deck of 32 cards formed by removing the sixes, fives, fours, threes and two from each suit in a standard 52-card deck.

plain suit A suit that is not the trump suit.

preference The name of a game and the hearts suit in that game.

proprieties Rules governing players' behaviour during card games, especially with regard to communication between partners.

rank The position of cards or suits in order of sequence. Cards are usually ranked within their suits with higher-ranking cards having higher values than lower-ranking cards. Suits are sometimes also ranked in the same way with some suits having higher values than others.

rearhand In Skat and others, the dealer.

reserve In solitaire games, cards that are available for play to the layout other than cards in any stock or discard piles. Reserves usually make it easier to complete a solitaire game because they give the player more options for possible play.

revoke Failing to follow suit when required to do so by the rules.

rubber In Contract bridge, a set of three games.

rubicon In Rubicon bezique and Piquet, the minimum points that the loser of a deal must reach to avoid his opponent gaining a bonus. A player who fails to reach that limit is said to be 'rubiconed'.

sequence A set of cards of the same suit that are in ranking order.

skat The name of a game and two cards dealt to the table in that game.

slam When one player or team wins all the tricks in a deal.

solitaire A card game for one player. Also called patience games.

start card In Cribbage and other games, a card from the undealt portion of the deck that is turned face-up before play begins and is used in combination with players' cards for the purposes of scoring.

stock Cards remaining after the deal that are used in subsequent stages of a game.

stripping Removing specific cards from a standard 52-card deck in order to form a playing deck with fewer cards.

suit One of the four classes or families that cards in a deck are divided into. The suits are spades, diamonds, clubs and hearts.

trick An element of play in which each player contributes one face-up card according to the rules of the game. Tricks are usually won by the player who contributes the highest-ranking card of the lead suit or the highest-ranking trump card.

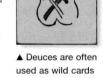

▲ Deuces are often used as wild cards

trump A suit that outranks all other suits. Cards from the trump suit usually outrank cards from non-trump suits even if the trump card has a lower face value.

upcard A card that is dealt face-up to the centre of the table, rather than to a specific player, or a card that is turned face-up from the top of a stock. Upcards are often used to determine trump suits.

undertrick In Contract bridge and other trick-taking games, tricks less than the number of tricks bid.

vole In the game of Ecarté, winning all five tricks.

vulnerability In Contract bridge, a partnership is said to be vulnerable if it has won a game and non-vulnerable if it has not.

widow A set of cards dealt to the table rather than a specific player. A widow often contains the same number of cards as the regular hands dealt to the players.

wild card A card that may be used instead of any other card. Jokers or deuces are commonly used as wild cards.

Need to know more?

There is a vast range of information available to anyone interested in finding out more about card games, particularly if you have access to the internet. The websites and publications listed below are portals to more detailed information. Bridge is the only card game that has national and international ruling bodies.

Internet resources: General

Card Games: very comprehensive archive of card game rules
www.pagat.com

Card Games Directory: host of links for all aspects of card game playing
www.card-games-directory.com

Card Game Rules: collection of rules for the most popular card games plus links to online gaming resources
www.cardgamerules.homestead.com

Historic Card Games: rules for some fascinating ancient card games
www.davidparlett.co.uk/histocs

Thanos Card Games: large collection of free card-playing software
www.geocities.com/thanoscardgames

The House of Cards: huge archive of links to free and commercial card-playing software
www.thehouseofcards.com

The International Playing-Card Society: organisation dedicated to the history of playing cards
www.i-p-c-s.org

Internet resources: Specific games

American Contract Bridge League
www.acbl.org

Beginner's Blackjack
www.beginnersblackjack.com

Cribbage Corner
www.splange.freeserve.co.uk/cribbage.html

Euchre Headquarters
http://users.stargate.net/~keyz

Solitaire Central
www.solitairecentral.com

Solitaire Game Guide
www.solitairegameguide.com

World Bridge Federation: including links to administrative divisions and member countries' sites
office@worldbridge.org
www.worldbridge.org

Equipment

Bishop Games Ltd.
32 City Arcade, Coventry, CV1 3HW
www.bishopgames.co.uk

Compendia Traditional Games and Puzzles
10 The Market, Greenwich, London, SE10 9HZ
www.compendia.co.uk

Masters Traditional Games
www.mastersgames.com

The Game Cabinet: includes listings for games shops all over the world
www.gamecabinet.com

Uncles Games.com
www.unclesgames.com

Magazines

Bridge Magazine
The London Bridge Centre
Chess & Bridge Ltd, 369 Euston Road, London NW1 3AR
www.bridgemagazine.co.uk

The Bridge World
The Bridge World, PO Box 299, Scarsdale, NY 10583, USA
mail@bridgeworld.com
www.bridgeworld.com

Index

Collins need to know?

Want to know about other popular subjects and activities?
Look out for further titles in Collins' practical and accessible
Need to Know? series.

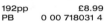

192pp   £8.99
PB   0 00 718031 4

192pp   £8.99
PB   0 00 718037 3

192pp   £7.99
PB   0 00 718038 1

192pp   £8.9
PB   0 00 7189032 2

192pp   £6.99
PB   0 00 719080 8

192pp   £8.99
PB   0 00 719091 3

192pp   £8.99
PB   0 00 719063 8 8

192pp   £8.9
PB   0 00 719088 3

Forthcoming titles:

Birdwatching
DIY
Drawing & Sketching
Stargazing
Weddings
French
Italian

Spanish
Kama Sutra
Dog Training
Knots & Splices
World Atlas
World Factfile

To order any of these titles,
please telephone **0870 787
1732**. For further information
about all Collins books, visit our
website: **www.collins.co.uk**